FORGERY, PERJURY, AND AN ENORMOUS FORTUNE

"No one with money dies without heirs."

—LATE W. BARTON LEACH
PROFESSOR, HARVARD LAW SCHOOL

Distributed by Persea Books

BEACH HAMPTON PRESS

FORGERY, PERJURY, AND AN ENORMOUS FORTUNE

2,303 CLAIMANTS TO THE ELLA WENDEL ESTATE (1931)

Mervin Rosenman

Printed in the United States of America
First Edition
Cover illustration: AP/Wide World Photos

In memory of

my Mother and my Uncle,

Judge Sam Rosenman

ACKNOWLEDGMENTS

My principal acknowledgment must be to Elihu Root, Jr., (1881–1967), a founding partner of the firm that, after several name changes, in 1931 was named Root, Clark & Buckner, for his instruction, "Never throw a file away." Thanks to his foresight—with the kind permission of its successor firm, Dewey, Ballantine, Bushby, Palmer & Wood and with the help of Miss Helene Lilly of its files office—I have had use of thirty-three cartons containing the prodigious research into fact and law that Root Clark performed in the Ella Wendel estate. I also am indebted to Dewey Ballantine for permission to quote from the *Bull (Bulletin)*, distributed weekly to Root Clark lawyers, describing the progress of the case.

I am grateful to Mrs. Judy V. Higens, Supervisor of the Record Room of the Surrogate's Court, New York County, who located and made available the six cartons containing the estate proceedings before Surrogate Foley. Due to the extraordinary efforts of Joseph Van Nostrand, Office of the Clerk of New York County, and Idilio Gracia Peña of the Municipal Records Center, the 1933 criminal trial transcript of

People of the State of New York vs. *Thomas Patrick Morris* was plucked from limbo. Nancy Bressler, Curator of the John Marshall Harlan papers in the Mudd Library at Princeton University, Fred A. Rubinstein, Esq., of Guggenheimer & Untermyer, and Morris Shilensky of Hays, St. John, Abramson & Heilbron kindly aided me in uncovering surviving records. The New York Public Library and Will Maslow, Esq., were invaluable in providing scrapbooks of newspaper clippings on the Wendel estate. Dr. Arthur Jones, the Librarian of Drew University, has graciously permitted me to use pictures from the Wendel family albums.

I am also indebted to Frank M. Foley, Esq., for information about his uncle, Surrogate Foley; to Edward M. K. Murray, who told me about his stepmother, Isabel Koss Murray, and the disposition of the Irvington property; to Mrs. Gertrude Swope who typed the manuscript; to Elisa Petrini for editorial help and to Nancy Etheredge for the design of the book.

Special thanks are due to my old friend, Joe Iseman, who first suggested to me that the Ella Wendel case would be a fit subject for a book.

Certainly I owe thanks to the lawyers connected with the Wendel estate: their recollections, evoked in my interviews, appear throughout the book and give the story its character and color. Four of those who were intimately involved have reviewed the manuscript for me. However, any errors of fact or judgment are solely my responsibility.

M.R.

New York City, 1984

1.

ELLA WENDEL DIES

Ella Wendel [is] Manhattan's land-richest individual.
TIME, AUGUST 4, 1930

During the 1920s, sightseeing buses would regularly stop at 442 Fifth Avenue, at the corner of Thirty-ninth Street, for the "House of Mystery." It was the only residence left in an area of business buildings, with all its windows shuttered and the front door heavily barred. The guides would tell of Ella, the recluse who lived there alone except for the servants and her dog, Tobey, and of her huge fortune, her bizarre life-style, and her curious history. Next to her house was an empty lot, used principally for Tobey's exercising, which the guides called the "$2 million dogrun." Gaping, the out-of-towners swallowed it all avidly.

A later affidavit would describe her as:

> a wizened, old and infirm woman. Her clothing was shabby and she wore but one dress, faded black turning into green with

> years of usage. She wore high button shoes, a blouse and invariably an old fashioned guimpe [a lace vest]. On her little knob of hair she wore a black ribbon. A sailor hat with a bow and black ribbon completed her appearance. However, no matter how sunny the day, she always wore rubbers. There was evidence she was far from clean.
>
> She spent more time on her dog than others do on their children. She had a number of dogs, all named Tobey, ever since she was a girl.
>
> When a dog was about to die she would call in her contractor to have an underground vault constructed. The vault would be dampproof and waterproof, with a concrete slab on top. It took four men to lift it, and there was room for one casket in it. The caskets were two-inch oak, with room for a white satin pillow. All the furnishings were of brass and of the best quality and the box was painted and varnished.
>
> The dog would be appropriately buried and the grave marked with a tombstone inscribed with the birth and death of the dog. The testatrix left notes with the coffin.

While the notes were never dug up, there can be little doubt that they were addressed by Ella to whatever Supreme Being would preside at the canine Armageddon, sifting out the souls of dogs before his judgment seat, urging him to send the souls of the seventeen prior Maltese poodle Tobeys to the good place.

When Ella Virginia Von Echtzel Wendel died, on March 13, 1931, at the age of seventy-eight, she left an estate appraised, even at the depths of the Great Depression, at $36 million—more than $200 million today—of choice real estate, mainly in New York City. The combination of an eccentric recluse leaving an enormous fortune, the unusual Wendel family, and an unfortunate (and untrue) statement by Charles Koss, the family lawyer, that she had "left no heirs" was to the newspapers and the wire services as kerosene to an arsonist.

There had been no juicy will-contest, involving millions, since the Jay Gould estate some years before. Throughout the United States and abroad, newspapers told almost daily of the Wendel fortune, varying at the whim of the reporter from $40 to $100 million, just begging to be claimed.

Who has not had the fantasy of a rich and unknown relative dying and leaving him a fortune that would enable him to end a humdrum life and to enjoy one of luxury? Twenty three hundred and three persons tried to get their hands on Ella's fortune, by hook or by crook. In the latter category were:

- Thomas Patrick Morris, a "nephew," who produced a forged marriage certificate, a forged will and two forged letters and, after a sensational hearing in the Surrogates' Court, had his claim disallowed. His claim bore similarity to the Tichborne Peerage imposter in England in the 1870s, as the newspapers pointed out. In a criminal trial thereafter he was convicted of conspiracy to defraud Ella's estate and sentenced to thirty-three months in the penitentiary.
- Some West Virginia claimants who erected an altered tombstone with altered birth and death dates of an ancestor to make their claim seem genuine.
- Some Illinois claimants who produced letters written in 1836 and 1841 by Ella's father. But the letter paper was proved to have been purchased at Woolworth's and manufactured not earlier than 1930.
- Some Maryland claimants, who faked two cards of ancient marriage records, dated 1819, and planted them in the files of the State Land Office.
- "Recipients" of three forged "Good Samaritan" letters, allegedly from Ella, her brother, and her grandfather, to some Illinois "relatives," promising them Ella's entire estate.
- Joseph Kuderma, an Austrian specialist in artificially aging documents, who on his arrest in Vienna confessed to forgery of beautifully aged, yellow papers proving he was the heir.

- The Tennessee Dew sisters, who presented forged documents to show that their ancestor was also Ella's ancestor.

And all of these claims, plus hundreds of others, were given the widest newspaper publicity as the contest developed.

No one even hinted that Ella had ever enjoyed the pleasures of the bed, but there were claimants perfectly willing to ascribe illicit sexual relationships to her relatives to improve their chances.

- Her grandfather, Johann, had, after migrating to America, been married to Elizabeth Astor in what his family believed to be his only marriage. Not at all, claimants asserted. Two separate groups of claimants, one of fifty-three persons from Germany and the other an elderly Belgian woman, asserted two separate marriages before he left Europe, with children by at least one bigamous marriage. According to another group of Ossining and Schenectady claimants, her grandfather had fallen in love with Violet Wal Shinnecock, the daughter of the chief of the Shinnecock Indians on Long Island; Violet's brothers, Joe Bear Wal and Buck Skin Wal, had accompanied him on his fur trapping and purchasing expeditions up the Hudson River and into Canada. From this misalliance, perhaps according to tribal betrothal rites or perhaps not, there was born a half-brother to Ella's father and his descendants demanded their due.

- Her father, John D., was accused of fathering an illegitimate child in New York by one Sarah Saltsman, who was then sent back to Indiana to have the child and live there; a claim was made by the issue of what was alleged to be an illegitimate half-brother of Ella.

- Her brother, John G., was alleged to have entered into a clandestine marriage and the child, Thomas Patrick Morris, made claim to be the sole heir of Ella; another claimant stated that John G. had married her mother secretly in Greenwich, Connecticut.

- Two of her sisters allegedly had illegitimate children, one of them through an incestuous union with Ella's brother, John G.

The claimants against the estate were not limited to persons who had pretensions to relationship with Ella. Indeed, many were charities, which Ella had disdained during her lifetime. Among them was:

> 1/2/33
> Claim of $13,654,942.48 against the estate of the late Miss Ella Virginia von E. Wendel as a bequest to assist our cause as a memorial. It is many days past due, as it was decided in conference with the late dear one not far back. As it is the 1st day of the year, we must collect. To start the year right, we expect a check by return mail. Fifteen days is all that can be allowed in this transaction.
> Don't forget, and thanking you, we remain,
> Rev. G. A. Galloway
> Fairfield, Illinois

There is no evidence of any negotiation between the Reverend and the representatives of Ella's estate.

Other extravagant claims poured in.

Katherine Murray of Harlingen, Texas, claimed Ella had agreed to pay for her home and her son's education, totaling $8,000. Elsie Wiersig of Chicago alleged that she was entitled to $11 million but could offer no rationale. A Joplin, Missouri, woman, Mary Richardville, asserted her right to the entire estate, while Hilda Smith of Great Britain claimed only $100 million as her legacy. A more modest sum was claimd by R. H. Sindle, administrator of the estate of Grace G. Sindle, who sought $3,500 as the balance due on a loan of $5,000 to Ella's father, John D. Wendel, in 1869 of which $1,500 was repaid in 1878. Mr. Sindle was informed that the statute of limitations on collecting the outstanding amount had expired more than fifty years before.

And finally a claimant alleged that when Ella's grandfather came to America in 1798, he absconded with the funds of a business in Altona, his home town. Alleging descent from his wronged partner, the claimant wanted his share of the Wendel fortune created by this nestegg. He, too, was told that the statute of limitations barred claims almost 140 years old.

The legal proceedings to settle the Wendel estate would last two years and would engage the services of:

- the most eminent Surrogate in New York (the Surrogate's Court handles probate of wills and the administration of estates, among other matters);
- two young lawyers, one of whom was to become an Associate Justice of the United States Supreme Court and the other Chief Judge of the prestigious U.S. Court of Appeals for the Second Circuit;
- one of the foremost civil liberties lawyers in the United States and one of the most eminent senior trial lawyers in New York City;
- other young lawyers, then in their twenties, who thereafter became senior partners in distinguished law firms or had eminent careers in large corporations or in communal organizations.

From these ingredients a juicy stew was concocted, the Ella Wendel will contest, that became an international cause célèbre.

2.

ELLA'S WEALTH AND LIFE-STYLE

Andrew Carnegie, the first J. Pierpont Morgan, Russell Sage, and many others accounted extremely wealthy did not leave as much as the little spinster of 442 Fifth Avenue.
NEW YORK WORLD-TELEGRAM
APRIL 29, 1931

"Ella Wendel was a high-grade moron."
STATEMENT OF ELLA'S DENTIST

When Ella Wendel died she owned real property assessed for estate tax purposes—(assessments that are always lower than the fair market value) at almost $30 million dollars.

WENDEL NEW YORK PROPERTIES	
442–6 Fifth Avenue	$4,548,000
38 Grand Street	20,000
40 Grand Street	20,000
5 Ninth Avenue	15,000
24 Thompson Street	13,000
14–20 Little West Twelfth Street (land only)	41,500
12 Little West Twelfth Street	16,000
70 West Fifty-first Street (land only)	20,000
1 Beaver Street (land only)	180,000
175 Broadway	550,000
70 West Fifty-first Street (land only)	100,000
573 Third Avenue	40,000
567 Third Avenue	66,000
Five other parcels in Irvington	147,000
79–89 Avenue D	78,000
157 Avenue C	17,500
53 Beekman Street	75,000
49 Ann Street	37,000
17 Avenue D	17,500
324 E. Third Street	12,000
181 Broadway	426,000
705 Broadway	65,000
45 Bond Street	30,000
73–81 Maiden Lane	600,000
386 Columbus Avenue	40,050
83½ Division Street	36,000
15 Essex Street	40,000
26–28 Thompson Street	67,500
225 Grand Street	23,000
405 Grand Street	35,000
815 Greenwich Street	15,000
144 Hester Street	23,000
213 and 215 Lewis Street (land only)	15,000
784 Lexington Avenue	150,000
55 Maiden Lane	170,000
119 Mulberry Street	23,000
513 and 515 Seventh Avenue	320,000
519 Seventh Avenue	400,000
521–527 Seventh Avenue and 141–151 West Thirty-eighth Street (land only)	1,750,000
53 Spring Street	37,500
118 Sullivan Street	24,000
67 and 69 Washington Street	70,000
246 West Broadway	10,000
329 West Broadway	22,000
457–461 West Broadway	115,000
381 and 383 West Twenty-sixth Street	43,000

1395,1397, 1398 Broadway, 129–30 West Thirty-eighth Street	1,500,000
529–35 Seventh Avenue	3,383,000
49 Canal Street	27,000
31–33 Mercer Street	70,000
1–3 Ninth Avenue	27,000
7 Ninth Avenue	26,000
95 Grand Street	21,000
8 Little West Twelfth Street	15,500
10 Little West Twelfth Street	15,500
21–23 Union Square (land only)	200,000
50 Spring Street (land only)	20,000
Cooper House and grounds, Quoque, Long Island	20,000
534 West Street (land only)	27,000
1633–39 Broadway	1,144,881
561–563 Third Avenue 203–05 East Thirty-seventh Street	160,000
Estate at Irvington	100,000
60-2-4 Avenue D	33,000
78 Avenue D	12,000
151 Avenue C	19,500
51 Beekman Street	78,000
55 Beekman Street	80,000
341 West Forty-sixth Street	23,500
529 and 531 West Fiftieth Street	55,000
99 and 101 William Street	275,000
560–564 Seventh Avenue and 203–205 West Fortieth Street	1,020,000
1639–1649 Broadway 211–229 West Fiftieth Street	2,175,300
1900–1908 Broadway	657,000
584–590 Eighth Avenue	260,000
865–867 Canal Street	72,000
81 Division Street	30,000
13 Essex Street	46,000
147 Fulton and 22 Ann Streets	225,000
231–235 Centre and 158–62 Grand Sts (land only)	109,500
407 Grand Street	56,000
817 Greenwich Street	16,000
289–301 Hudson Street and 294–330 Spring Street	121,000
783 Lexington Avenue	165,000
8 Maiden Lane	175,000
98 Grand Street	16,000
878 Pearl Street	17,000
517 Seventh Avenue	288,000
144–150 West Thirty-eighth Street	500,000

Property	Value
51 Ann Street	37,000
322 East Third Street	9,000
150 Broadway (land only)	1,000,000
703 Broadway	65,000
711 Broadway	74,000
1385–91 Broadway, 136–42 West Thirty-eighth Street (land only)	2,028,000
1401–09 Broadway 34–48 West Thirty-ninth Street	1,760,000
1625 Broadway	240,000
1876–80 Broadway 11 West Sixty-second and 9 West Sixty-first Streets	1,376,000
47–49 West Sixty-third Street	240,000
825 Sixth Avenue	60,000
1014–1018 Sixth Avenue and 32 and 34 West Thirty-eighth Street	466,650
37 Spruce Street	50,000
182 Third Avenue	22,500
370 West Street	26,500
327 West Broadway	22,000
344–354 West Broadway	80,000
352 West Eleventh Street	10,000
335 and 337 West Twenty-sixth Street	43,000
101–133 West Fourth Street	380,000
87 and 89 William Street	100,000
188 William Street	36,000

In addition, she owned real property in Brooklyn and in other states worth more than $450,000; she had $1.9 million cash in banks, and bonds and securities worth $2.9 million.

Notwithstanding her wealth, she lived the life of a penny-pinching recluse, resisting all change, maintaining things as they had been during her childhood. Her five-story house at 442 Fifth Avenue had been built, at a cost of $5,000, in what was then a wilderness, in the early 1850s when Abe Lincoln was still an unknown prairie lawyer in Illinois. It had no elevator or dumbwaiter; the staircases were very steep, in the style of the era; and the kitchen still had the original hooded stove fueled with coal brought from the basement in scuttles. The furniture purchased in the 1850s had never been replaced.

The house had one large zinc bathtub ten feet long and four feet high. When the question of replacing it with one of porcelain arose, John G., Ella's brother, put his foot down. "That old zinc tub was good enough for ma and pa and it's good enough for us." The house was lighted with gas lamps and candles, because the family believed they were easier on the eyes. Ella too refused to bring in that new-fangled electricity, except in the dining room, where the old crystal chandelier was wired, and she had no telephone.

Once, Koss, the family lawyer, pointed out that the land on which the house and the dogrun existed could be sold for $4 million; the lost interest on that amount plus the real estate taxes Ella had to pay amounted to more than $1,000 per day. He sent a real estate broker to see Ella: he promised her a penthouse and a private elevator in a new building if she would sell. Horrified, Ella replied, "Why, you want to buy our house and the shoes off our feet." After Ella's death, Annie Gavin, her personal maid, quoted her as wondering "why such families as the Vanderbilts, Bloodgoods, Goulds, and Goelets live in hotels and apartments instead of their own houses."

The house at 442 Fifth Avenue had 157 trunks of family effects—clothing, trinkets, and fabrics—which Ella spent much time and effort arranging and rearranging, attempting to recapture the happier days when her sisters and brother were alive and living a family life with her parents. To a family friend, William Geisse, she wrote, "I wish some of the family would rise up and help me with the trash." There were also eight safes, the combinations of which were hidden throughout the house; one contained overdue coupon bonds dated as far back as 1840, another held an extremely modest amount of family jewelry. When Ella took long walks with Tobey during the night, she would leave the side door of the house unlocked, saying, "There is nothing here for burglars to take."

Ella had been educated, along with her sisters, with private lessons from frauleins and governesses. She was by all accounts a very simple, timid, shy person, without wit or charm. Her mind was childish and undeveloped. Her brother would insist that William Lopez Diaz or some other person from the family real estate office have breakfast with him because he could not endure the peasantlike conversation of Ella and her sisters. Presumably she never attended a ball, never flirted with, or even had, a gentleman caller and, given her abhorrence of alcohol, never sipped a cocktail. Even personal hygiene was beyond her limited capacity. Ella's dentist stated that there was dirt behind her ears and her scalp was encrusted!

Since meat was too expensive, Ella ate mainly vegetables, grown on the forty acres of the Wendel family country place at Irvington-on-Hudson. It was her favorite place. As Annie Gavin recounted it, this was due in part to the fact that the "soot that came from the soft coal burned in New York made Tobey's coat dirty." Or, as Ella wrote to a friend in 1928:

> *Our puppy does not like winter. He has no freedom as he cannot be off the lead in New York City. Streets were never so dirty as this year. Annie brings the dog in with legs and feet as black as coal. It soils his coat on the side. Three pails of water, soda and soap does not clean it. He should be carried over crossings but no one will do that but myself.*

Irvington was no less antique than 442 Fifth. The house was not insulated, and it, too, had no telephone or electricity; water was drawn by an old-fashioned hand pump. Ella stayed there from April to November, when she was forced by the cold to retreat to 442. At a court hearing Joseph Fallon, the postmaster of Irvington, testified that in 1930 he had suggested to Ella that she install an oil-burning furnace so she could live there all year round. Ella replied she couldn't afford it.

After her brother and four of her sisters died—leaving only Georgiana, in a mental institution, and Rebecca, who was blind and later incompetent—Ella became even more of a recluse. In 1928 she wrote to a friend, "I would not have a radio in the house for a million dollars." She never read newspapers, never went to the theater or to the opera, and refused to receive old friends who called on or wanted to visit her. As she told one of them, who wanted her children to visit Ella,

> It would be nice to see Isoline and Warren but I assure you the dog would be annoyed dreadfully and as soon as anyone comes he bites the mats, sofa covers, chairs, tablecloth, etc. unless I shut him in a room on the 2d floor. He would not rest all night if anyone was rooming here.

She did not live in the modern world, either mentally or physically.

Dogs had always been the principal focus in her life. As far back as 1898 she wrote to the ASPCA:

> *No doubt you read this article in yesterday's Herald, but in case you did not see it you will oblige me by reading it. It is anything but pleasant to have a disagreeable encounter with a vicious animal & I am quite sure if you had to wrestle with people's dogs on the streets as I have this winter you would do all you could to have a law passed that dogs must be led or muzzled and you would* see *that it was* enforced also. *Who wants to have his face disfigured for life! I know that nothing would compensate me, not even if the person laid down his life.*

But now the succession of Tobeys became her sole interest. The current Tobey would sleep in her bedroom in a small

Ella and Tobey

four-poster bed that matched Ella's exactly. At nine A.M. she would take him for a long walk—the dogrun next to 442 was flagstoned to prevent him from becoming muddy. Then Tobey would be bathed, and the two would breakfast together, with Ella herself cooking Tobey's liver or chop. Another long walk followed in the afternoon. At dinner, Tobey would eat with her in the dining room off his own small brass table, complete with velvet tablecloth and napkin. Afterward she would bathe him again and they would take another walk, then retire early and she would talk to the dog until they both fell asleep. Once, to tease Ella, a villager in Irvington asked her at what price she would sell the dog. At this, Ella flared up and exclaimed with violent passion, "All the money in the world could not buy my Tobey." Ella would tell and retell this story to others, in semi-hysterical outrage. Ella's dentist recalled that on her visits to him Ella talked of nothing but Tobey. She signed her letters, "With love from Tobey and me." On several occasions, Tobey became ill and the vet suggested he remain indoors. So Ella got a child's perambulator and wheeled him around the house, and after his recovery, even around the Irvington property, to the amusement of her neighbors.

Ella's obsessive concern extended to her fat old carriage horses as well. When her longtime coachman, Richard Lundy, died in 1929, Ella feared for the horses' care under a successor coachman, or in the event of her death, at the hands of the knackers. So she had the horses put down and buried in the animal graveyard in Irvington. With the horses gone, a car was purchased for Irvington, but it was never brought to New York City.

Not having a telephone required Ella to write to tradespeople. She would send a letter to Wanamakers department store to buy a dish towel, or to the confectioner's to buy a bar of chocolate. When she wanted to go to her dentist on Forty-second Street, three blocks from 442, she would write Rebecca's chauffeur in Quogue, Long Island—a hundred miles away. Two days later he would arrive to convey her the three blocks and then would return to Quogue. When her dentist's assistant suggested she call a taxi, Ella replied, "Why, I never thought of that."

This extravagant use of the chauffeur was hardly typical of Ella. She would haggle over the servants' wages and complain about how much food they ate, argue over bills from tradespeople and the prices quoted by salesclerks. She had been in the habit of giving each of the servants $10 and several changes of underwear twice a year. Two years before her death, she discontinued this practice, telling them, "I can't do it any more, I am too poor." When beggars came to the door, Ella would have the servants say she was out. She mended her own clothes and the carpets in the house to cover the worn spots. Her appearance was so shabby that once when she went to Tiffany to buy a silver teapot as a present, the salesgirl, after looking her over, suggested she go to Macy's.

Ella would have been pleased by her funeral, for it was as sparse and frugal as her life. She was a small woman, weighing eighty pounds or so, and her casket was as small and inexpensive as possible. It was barely larger than a child's, the rubbernecks noted as they waited on the sidewalk, watching the last of the Wendels depart from what the newspapers were calling The House Without Children.

This cheese-paring, nay miserliness, was compounded by Ella's eccentricities and complete failure to comprehend the size of her fortune. Here was ample material for a will contest based on her lack of capacity to make a will.

3.

ELLA'S FAMILY

"Buy, never mortgage and never sell real estate."
WENDEL FAMILY MOTTO

It was the custom of poor immigrants who became wealthy to seek aristocratic ancestors, so the Wendels had engaged a genealogist—at cut-rate prices, we must presume—to find theirs. They were confident that their forbears had marched with kings in Europe. One of Ella's given names, von Echtzel, reflected this patrician "lineage"—a pretension to the Prussian nobility utterly without foundation.

Rebecca, Ella's sister, had left genealogical notes that one Hans Balthorzen Wendel Von Echtzel received his act of legitimation from Charles V in Valladolid, Spain, on September 21, 1523, which permitted him to wear a tournament helmet. On February 10, 1663, George Wendel Von Echtzel, whose family was traceable back to 1495, was created a Knight of the Holy

John D. Wendel

Roman Empire of Swabia. His coat of arms signified boldness, bodily strength, and proficiency in arms. Had there been one more generation of Wendels after Ella, a coat of arms would probably have been created; it might have shown portions of the family real estate and, in Latin, their inviolate lease provision *Tenant must make his own repairs*.

Ella's grandfather, Johann Gottlob Matthias Wendel, was born in 1767 in the small town of Altona, then part of the Kingdom of Denmark but later to become part of Schleswig-Holstein in Germany. At the age of thirty-one, he emigrated to America. Shortly after his arrival he had the good fortune to meet John Jacob Astor, who had emigrated some years before from Walldorf, Germany (hence the name of the most luxurious hotel in America). Astor was engaged in the fur trade, buying skins from trappers, and Johann became his partner. Astor had already begun to buy New York real estate with the fur profits, and he soon persuaded Johann to do the same.

Mary Ann the Amiable

Eventually Johann became friendly enough to marry John Jacob's half-sister, Elizabeth Astor (age twenty-six), in New York City on August 4, 1799. They had three children: George Heinrich Wendel was born in 1806 and died in infancy; Elizabeth Wendel was born in 1810 and died in 1820; but their first child, born in 1800, John Daniel Wendel, lived to carry on the family line.

In 1834, "John D." married a Maryland woman who must have been a veritable paragon of goodness; she is described in the Wendel family Bible as "Mary Ann Dew the Amiable." Mary Ann came from distinguished stock. Her grandfather, General Tobias Emerson Stansbury, was a hero of the War of 1812 and had received a grant of land in Baltimore County for services to his country; he had settled and flourished there during a long life of ninety-two years. His daughter, Harriet, born to the General and Mary Buffington, married James C. Dew, and Mary Ann was born of that union.

Mary Ann the Amiable and John D. had eight children:

John Gotttlieb	1835–1914
Henrietta	1837–1876
Mary	1839–1922
Rebecca (Swope)	1842–1930
Augusta	1845–1912
Josephine	1849–1914
Georgiana	1850–1929
Ella	1853–1931

After Johann's death in 1841, John D. continued to buy real estate as the city expanded northward. Then, in 1860, he moved his entire household to Germany so his only son could avoid serving in the Civil War. It was an extreme precaution—considering the family's wealth, he easily could have bought a substitute to serve in his son's stead.

In 1876 John D. died, and that son, John G., would become the patriarch of the family. He had attended Heidelberg University and was graduated from Columbia—an educational background he denied his sisters—and he was fluent in German, Italian, and French. Like Ella, he too had his personal quirks. Just as Ella wore rubbers 365 days a year, John G. carried an umbrella, rain or shine, winter and summer. He believed that most diseases were contracted through the feet, so he wore shoes with gutta-percha soles one inch thick, projecting one inch on all sides, to insulate him from the germs in the ground. He also believed that dye in fabrics was dangerous to health. All of his suits were made of wool shorn from black sheep in Scotland and then specially woven for his tailor, who used as a model a suit John G. had purchased at the end of the Civil War. Whenever he needed suits he sent the model to the tailor in its original box from forty years before, which had to be returned with the model. He ordered eighteen suits at a

John G., Ella's brother

time, so they could be distributed evenly between his homes at Quogue, Irvington, and 442 Fifth Avenue. But he had only one hat, which he wore until it fell apart, for each season being varnished a bright, shiny black.

His business life was equally eccentric. He would issue leases for a term of three years only. Electric signs were forbidden on Wendel properties, and theaters and saloons were taboo. Even after John G.'s death, the proscription of liquor continued, and the newspapers told of the Wendel office holding up a million-dollar lease for over two weeks, until the tenant guaranteed that the first-aid kit in the building would not contain more than one pint of whiskey. John G. would not install a telephone; he had disliked them ever since a messenger from a candy store opposite 442 once summoned him for an emergency call. When he arrived at the store to receive it, he was greeted by a process server, who had devised this ruse.

His greatest obsession was money, expanding his already

princely fortune. He was always at his office, busying himself with minutiae that should have been left to clerks. He collected rents and negotiated leases himself. His sister Mary wrote in June 1902 to him from Quogue, urging him to enjoy himself more. John replied by relating tales of New York families who had once been rich but had become paupers because

> they were not on the spot looking closely after their property interests . . . It behooves someone to be on hand to stick up for one's rights and to resist injustices under guise of lawful charges and expenses and in this way prevent, as far as possible, riches taking wings and lodging in someone's else's pocket and strongbox and we become poorer and poorer like the Kinglands [once wealthy] and now so impoverished. Now you have the answer to your letter of wonderment why I do not hasten away from town and leave riches to take wings just as our friends have done to their sorrow and regret.

Fees paid to lawyers were an especial peeve. He would die without a will, rather than pay his lawyer to draw one.

He did not wear his knowledge of languages lightly. He would issue dinner invitations to 442 in German, Italian, or French, depending on the type of cooking that was to be served, or occasionally in Latin if the recipient knew the language. But during the last ten or fifteen years of his life, he became, as the newspapers said, the Millionaire Recluse of Fifth Avenue. In 1907 he refused a dinner invitation:

> Refraining by reason of varying health by temperament and disinclination as well from participating in social entertainments, diversions, and similar functions, I feel in duty to myself and in the interests of those dependent on me, that I may be pardoned answering to an unswerving resolution to decline acceptance of entertainment in however alluring and attractive guise an invitation to dine out *en ville* may present. Craving your gracious in-

> dulgence for this humble admission on my part, I beg to subscribe myself with expressions of high regard and sincere appreciation of your kindly courtesy to your most obedient servant.

If his dinner-table conversation was like his correspondence, his becoming a recluse is readily understandable.

John G. was tyrannical with his seven sisters. They were forbidden jewelry and forced to make their own clothes (with ankle-length skirts, high collars, and long sleeves) out of expensive black cloth, which was then to be worn to shabbiness. As adults, they wore the round sailor hats popular in the 1870s. Male visitors were discouraged because they might become suitors and, in time, husbands, which would fractionate the Wendel realty interests. No automobiles or public entertainments such as theater or opera were permitted to the residents of 442—John G. called them frivolous and too expensive. In the interest of economy, chickens were kept in the dogrun and the laundry was hung out to dry, to the distress of the Union League Club across the street.

Henrietta, the second oldest, died early, at age thirty-nine. Another sister, Augusta, was committed to an institution as an incompetent for the last forty years of her life. Mary and Josephine were strange and eccentric but caused John G. no trouble. Josephine, according to a newspaper account, lived in a dream world in one of the houses in Quogue, imagining that the Wendel home was filled with noisy and happy children, with whom she would talk, sing, and play. She would have the servants set six places for lunch, and as each course was served, she would change seats, pretending she was each of the guests in turn. She and Mary died as quietly as they lived.

Georgiana was gay and rebellious. She had a history of paranoia and had been institutionalized as early as 1896. Then in 1903, without telling her brother, she ran away to Europe and remained there five years, part of which time was spent in a sanitarium in Kiel, Germany. On her return she was permitted to return to the family, broken in spirit, where she lived with a series of nurse-companions. Finally, in 1919, she was committed as insane to Bloomingdale Hospital; there she remained for the ten years until her death—a death all her friends thought had occurred long before. Her sojourn in Europe would result in the claim of one Meta Strauch to be her illegitimate daughter—a claim that would cost Ella's estate hundreds of thousands of dollars to prove fraudulent. If John G. were then alive, he would have recoiled violently at the expense but felt fully vindicated in the correctness of the manner in which he insisted his sisters should live their lives.

Rebecca, called Beckie by her sisters, was not gay but was even more rebellious. According to observers, she was the prettiest and brightest of the sisters. She was not reclusive and she escaped John G.'s control. For over forty years, she busied herself with charitable works. Then at the age of sixty-one—alas, beyond childbearing age—she defied John G. and married Luther Swope, a tutor to wealthy children, and, according to the contemporaneous accounts, "a Christian gentleman of culture and standing." Swope was related to the Vicar of Trinity Church, and Rebecca had met Swope there; thereafter John G. kept his other sisters away from religious services. The Swopes lived at 248 Central Park West in New York City and in the summer used one of the Quogue, Long Island, houses.

After John G.'s death in 1914, Rebecca became the head of the family. When in Quogue, she received messengers, checks, and mail from the family office at 175 Broadway. When in New York, twice a week she would ride downtown on the elevated to cope with affairs. The newspapers called her The Little Old Lady of Realty Row.

She continued the family adage of never selling real es-

Rebecca ("Beckie"), Ella's sister

tate. Once when she sold a strip of Brooklyn land, too narrow for erecting a building, to the adjacent landowner, her lawyers exacted a commitment from the purchaser not to record the deed during Rebecca's lifetime, lest a horde of real estate agents urging more sales descend on the family office. Mary and Ella admired Beckie deeply for her ability to cope.

Ten years before her death in 1930, Rebecca became blind—a secret hidden from the world—and she retired to Quogue. Even then she maintained her interest in church and missionary work, in orphans' homes, in the prevention of blindness, and with hospitals; she knew exactly what she wished to do with her fortune. As time passed, she, like her sisters, became incompetent, a fact also carefully concealed. During this period, there was no Wendel to run the family business. Ella and Rebecca gave powers of attorney to the trusted oldtime employees, and they, along with the attorney Koss, handled the sisters' affairs.

When Rebecca died in 1930, eight months before Ella, she left a gross estate of over $17 million; over $13 million in real estate was bequeathed to Ella, if she survived, and the balance of more than $3 million went to Rebecca's charities. These charities were almost identical to those named in Ella's will, despite Ella's known contempt for them—a coincidence not lost on the hopeful claimants of the vast Wendel fortune.

And with Ella's death there was no more Wendel family to buy and never sell real estate.

4.

ELLA'S WILL

"It's a great pity Mrs. S. [Rebecca Swope, her sister] has not got any things [sic] else on the brain but her will and 200 associations, or my will. If she wants to know my will *is nothing doing but I am forced into it, to get rid of people."*

LETTER TO WILLIAM DIAZ DATED JULY 21, 1923

The very day before writing this letter, Ella had signed her will. Koss had urged her to make one, at Rebecca's insistence, he claimed in a memorandum prepared after Ella's death. According to Annie Gavin, the faithful maid, Ella replied to Koss that she could not be bothered spending time on a will. Koss persisted. One day he came to 442 in early spring 1923, Annie related, and remained closeted with Ella in the library for a long afternoon. Finally Ella capitulated.

Or did she? Was the will truly her own? Was Ella competent to make a will at all? The document that emerged was as curious as its eccentric author.

The initial bequests were fairly routine. Executed in Irvington July 20, 1923, the will provided for cash bequests varying bettween $2,000 and $10,000 to five servants, bequests of parcels of real estate in Irvington to two servants, and modest gifts to the Dobbs Ferry Hospital and to Hamilton College. Ella's sterling silver tea set and tray from Tiffany were given to Isabel Koss. Ella then gave a parcel of real estate in New York City to her doctor and another to William Diaz, and she left the building at 175 Broadway, where the family office was located, to Stanley Shirk, Luther Swope's nephew, if he survived Rebecca.

Then came some surprising provisions. First, there was a bequest of the extremely valuable parcel at Fiftieth Street and Broadway, assessed at $2,175,000, to Rebecca for life and upon her death to the attorney, Koss. Another bequest was made to Koss's daughter, of the country family home in Irvington, valued at $100,000, along with the real estate at 1 Beaver Street in New York City, (assessed for $180,000 for the land alone.) The Standard Oil Company had erected a building that paid rent of $12,000 per year, which would provide Isabel with "a large income to properly maintain and care for the property [in Irvington]." The bequest of the Irvington home to Isabel Koss further provided:

> While I do not impose any binding condition . . . upon the devise to . . . Isabel Koss, it is my earnest wish . . . that said property not be disposed of by her . . . but be occupied by her as a residence . . . or [alternatively] that it be leased by her for residential purposes.

Here, as we will see, substantial problems as to the probate of the will emerge.

The New York City home at 442 Fifth Avenue was bequeathed (if Ella survived Rebecca, as she did) to the Drew

Theological Seminary, "as a memorial to my father, the late John D. Wendel," with the "earnest wish" that the Seminary retain, rather than sell, the property. Drew Theological Seminary (now Drew University) had an old connection with the family. Various memorial funds of $10,000 each were established at Drew on the deaths of Mary Ann the Amiable and of Ella's brothers and sisters. In view of this past—and, he devoutly hoped, future—generosity, Ezra Squier Tipple was extremely attentive to Ella and Rebecca. But Ella didn't like him. In a letter to Beckie in January 1923 she wrote:

> *I fancy the Tipples make sure they get their share of the funds for the Drew Theological Seminary, that is why they feel obliged to send books and papers . . . I never hear of anyone leaving any thing to the Drew Seminary or of anyone who has benefited by it.*

The residue of the estate was to be divided into 200 parts, distributed as follows:

PARTS	INSTITUTIONS
35	Drew Theological Seminary
35	Board of Foreign Missions of the Methodist Episcopal Church for use in the Theological Seminary at Nankin [sic], China
35	New York Society for the Relief of Ruptured and Crippled
35	Flower Hospital
35	St. Christopher's Home for Children, Dobbs Ferry, New York

5	American Society for the Prevention of Cruelty to Animals
5	National Committee for the Prevention of Blindness
4	The Methodist Episcopal Church Home
3	Northfield Schools at East Northfield, Mass.
2	Presbyterian Hospital, New York City
2	National Kindergarten Association
2	Dobbs Ferry Hospital Association
1	Massachusetts Society for the Prevention of Cruelty to Animals
1	Trustees of the New York Annual Conference of the Methodist Episcopal Church

These generous bequests were peculiar because Ella always called charities that solicited contributions "grafters." The household servants unanimously agreed that in the last thirty years of her life Ella never went to church. Rev. Lee H. Ball, pastor of the Methodist church in Irvington, reported to Will Maslow that he once saw the clause in a Wendel lease: "None of our property is leased for churches, theatres or other forms of cheap amusements."

Ella had said of her will, "Make it like Beckie's," according to Koss's notes. Ella's charitable provisions did indeed parallel Rebecca's, with two significant differences. But it was very unlike "Beckie's will," under which Isabel and Koss received no bequests. And most important, Beckie did not execute her will until five months *after* Ella.

The executors named for Ella's will were Rebecca (who, of course, never served), Charles Koss, Stanley Shirk, and Isabel Koss. Yet Isabel had neither qualifications nor familiarity with the Wendels' affairs, and stood to receive huge executrix commissions from the estate. The choice of Isabel as an executrix provided additional ammunition for the threatened attack on the will.

Then, on February 29, 1939, Ella amended her will by a codicil. She revoked her prior legacy of $10,000 and a parcel of real estate in Irvington to Richard Lundy, her coachman, with a gift over to his son, Joseph, upon Richard's death—without giving any reason other than Richard had died. If Ella knew what this codicil meant, which is doubtful, she made a grave error, and Koss should have talked her out of it. The change would make Joseph Lundy, the son, a dangerous antagonist on the issue of her competence, in case the will was ever contested. There is evidence that Ella did not know what she had done, because she maintained friendly relations with Joseph until her death. Indeed, in 1930 Ella paid to repaint Joseph's house and continued to supply him with fresh milk, butter, and vegetables from Irvington. Mary Ehlinger, one of the maids, believed that Koss "greedily" induced Ella to revoke the bequest because the codicil then bequeathed that same parcel to Isabel.

And finally on June 13, 1929, she signed a second codicil increasing the amount of the bequest to Annie Gavin, the person she was closest to in the entire world, from $5,000 to $25,000.

But that leaves the curious incident of Tobey. In Arthur Conan Doyle's *Silver Blaze*, involving a racehorse abducted

The Wendel country home, Irvington, N.Y.

from the stable where there was a watchdog, Sherlock Holmes calls Watson's attention:

> "To the curious incident of the dog in the night time."
> "The dog did nothing in the night time" [says Watson].
> "That was the curious incident," remarked Holmes.

If this were truly Ella's will, what could account for her total failure to mention her precious Tobey? She made *no* designation of the person to care for him and *no* bequest of money for his support.

And there was still one more complication. The will and both codicils began, "I, Ella Virginia Von Echtzel Wendel, of Irvington, Westchester County . . ." The second codicil was dated less than two years before Ella's death; surely it seemed that her domicile—that is, her permanent residence—was thereby established beyond question. This expectation was destined not to be realized.

5.

BATTLE ARRAY OF LAWYERS

John M. Harlan was the best prepared lawyer who ever appeared before me.
SURROGATE JAMES A. FOLEY

What most states call the Probate Court is named the Surrogate's Court in New York; its presiding judge is called the Surrogate. Every other county in the state has one Surrogate, but New York County, with its large caseload—the destined Wendel battleground—has two. From 1920 to 1945, its principal Surrogate was James A. Foley, a judge of superior intellect, extremely learned in the law of probate, estates, and other matters handled by his court. He was six feet tall and slim, always smooth-shaven and wearing his pince-nez—a stiff and correct man, without much warmth. He was very stern and formal on the bench and only a little less so in his chambers. As Henry Friendly recalls, "If he had a sense of humor he kept it well disguised from me." Foley's consuming passion was golf, and magazines of the day had many pictures of his putting and chipping. He was held in very high regard by the Appellate Courts and it was axiomatic at the bar that his decisions were virtually never reversed.

The Proponent in the case—the firm preparing Ella's will and offering it for probate—was Thompson, Koss & Warren. Thompson, long since dead, had represented the Wendel family since the Civil War. Charles G. Koss, who at Ella's death was seventy-seven years old and suffered from heart trouble, had represented John G. and his seven sisters from 1876 until 1907, when a quarrel ruptured the association. As Koss later testified, "There was a difference of opinion. Neither would give way to the other. We were both stubborn and that ended the relationship." Koss did not vault back into the Wendel saddle until after John G. died in 1914; no surviving Wendel was as stubborn, so Koss remained the family lawyer. The third partner, Warren, was a younger, vigorous lawyer who was careful and meticulous in his work. The firm's chief associate was John Edmund Hewitt, the most brilliant intellect in the group, who would later become a partner and then a law professor.

Perhaps Warren and Hewitt originally thought they could handle the estate themselves, but the two thousand–odd claimants and the legal entanglements soon convinced them they needed help. They sought it from an experienced litigator, Emory R. Buckner, who had a large staff of lawyers—then about seventy—to draw on as specific issues arose. The firm selected was Root, Clark & Buckner, or "Root Clark," as it was commonly known in legal circles, who would aid in defending the will and in upholding the claims of the charities named as beneficiaries.

Buckner, then fifty-four years old, was the head of the

litigation department at Root Clark and had received wide publicity for his skill in the courtroom. Originally from Nebraska, he had attended Harvard Law School and established his practice in New York City. He served as Assistant District Attorney in New York County and from 1925 to 1927 as United States Attorney for the Southern District of New York. In that capacity, he vigorously and successfully prosecuted violators of the Prohibition laws. Buckner personally opposed Prohibition, nevertheless, he scrupulously enforced it.

Buckner's chief assistant at Root Clark was John Marshall Harlan, scion of a long line of distinguished lawyers that had graced the profession almost since the beginning of the Republic. His great-grandfather, James Harlan, was a Kentucky congressman and State Attorney General in the days when John Marshall was the Chief Justice of the United States Supreme Court. His son, born in 1833, was named John Marshall Harlan in honor of the Chief Justice; he too served as a distinguished and dynamic Justice of the Supreme Court, from 1877 to 1911. His son, John Maynard Harlan, became a prominent lawyer and public figure in Chicago. In turn, John Maynard passed on the illustrious name to his son, born in 1899, who would come to dominate the Ella Wendel case.

Harlan was graduated from Princeton University in 1920 and received a Rhodes Scholarship to study law at Balliol College, Oxford; there he took his degree, with first-class honors in Jurisprudence. Buckner hired him as an associate attorney at Root Clark in 1923, with the proviso that he spend his afternoons at New York Law School learning American law, so he could join the New York bar. Harlan soon proved his worth, and when Buckner became United States Attorney, he chose Harlan to be a chief lieutenant on his staff. When Buckner returned to Root Clark in 1927, Harlan remained his chief assistant and in 1931 was made a junior partner in the firm. He

Emory R. Buckner (right) and his assistant, John M. Harlan

would become one of the leading trial lawyers in New York. In 1954 he would serve as Judge of the Federal Court of Appeals, Second Circuit, and eight months later be appointed Associate Justice of the United States Supreme Court, a post he held with great distinction for seventeen years.

With Buckner, Harlan plunged into the Wendel case, and quickly distinguished himself—so much so that when Buckner suffered a slight stroke in March 1932, the Proponents and the attorneys for the charities retained him rather than replace him with a more experienced litigator. It was a judgment he brilliantly vindicated. His chief skills as a lawyer, along with his intellect, were his painstaking attention to detail and exhaustive preparation; his mastery of facts and ability to articulate them; and his skill in cross-examining witnesses. Even

Surrogate Foley noted his organization of evidence—Harlan prepared each paper in a separate folder, with arguments for its relevance, possible challenges to its admissibility, and a memorandum of law, prepared before the hearing, citing legal authorities in support of his position. He followed the same practice in reverse for items that he would expect his adversary to attempt to introduce in evidence. Everything flowed in orderly progression, and he allowed no fumbling by his assistants—the twenty-five young associates of Root Clark, then in their twenties, who worked at various times on the Wendel estate.

Among them was Henry J. Friendly, a Harvard College graduate, who placed first in his class at Harvard Law School; from 1927 to 1928 he had been law clerk to Justice Louis D. Brandeis. He joined Root Clark in 1928 and became a partner in 1936. Ten years later, he would become a partner in his own firm, Cleary, Gottlieb, Friendly & Hamilton. In 1959 he would be appointed Judge of the United States Court of Appeals for the Second Circuit, serve as Chief Judge from 1971 to 1973, and then become a Senior Judge.

Another young associate was Charles C. MacLean, who came to Root Clark in 1931 and would spend his entire legal career there, eventually becoming a senior partner in Dewey, Ballantine, where he practices today.

Working alongside the Root Clark contingent were the attorneys of the Residuary Charities. These fourteen charities, who would divide the bulk of the estate, were understandably eager to ensure that Ella's will be probated. The five greatest beneficiaries—Drew Theological Seminary, the Foreign Missions of the Methodist Church, the New York Society for Ruptured and Crippled, Flower Hospital, and the St. Christopher Home for Children—would each receive 35/200ths, or a total of 175/200ths of the residue. So, to aid in the effort, the lawyers for the five formed a committee, with George L. Shearer and Ben A. Matthews as principal members.

The opposition was formidable. There was a huge field of claimants to the fortune, an issue of competence, a question of undue influence—a quagmire of legal problems. Titillated by the sensationalist press, the public longed for a hint of scandal. And the principal attorneys contesting the validity of the will were Arthur Garfield Hays and Samuel Untermyer—two of the most famous, and most flamboyant, lawyers in New York.

Never one to shrink from the limelight, Hays, a vigorous fifty-year-old, had built his reputation on many civil liberties cases. Hays had received nationwide publicity for his role in the Sacco and Vanzetti case and, with Clarence Darrow and Dudley Field Malone, for opposing Willian Jennings Bryan in the Scopes "Monkey Trial" in Dayton, Tennessee. In time, he would defend the Scottsboro Boys and, from 1932 until his death in 1954, would serve as co-counsel for the American Civil Liberties Union (ACLU). Hays was a short man, who walked with a limp from a horseback-riding accident, with a warm, intense personality that attracted a vast number of celebrities. Friday night gatherings in his Greenwich Village home were attended by literary and entertainment notables.

Hays made some court appearances in the Wendel case and negotiated the ultimate settlement himself, but most of the legal work was done by other members of his firm, Hays, St. John, Abramson & Schulman—principally by John Schulman.

The bulk of the investigative work fell to Will Maslow, a young student about to be graduated from Columbia Law School in the spring of 1931. While attending law school, Maslow had worked full time as a reporter for the *New York Times* to help support his parents. Hays hired him, he said in his book *City Lawyer* (New York: Simon & Schuster, 1942), because "he needed us and we needed him." Although the usual starting salary for young lawyers at Wall Street firms was $2,400 per year, the Hays firm paid $10 per week. But because of his investigative experience, Maslow bargained for and received $25 per week. He later became successively general counsel, executive director, and again general counsel of the American Jewish Congress.

Hays's aide in the highly complicated settlement of the suit and the division of the monies was his former office boy, Morris Shilensky. A twenty-one-year-old employee in 1931, Shilensky attended law school at night and was admitted to the bar in 1933. He would become a senior partner of the Hays firm.

Hays decided the Wendel estate was too complicated for his small firm to handle. So he persuaded Samuel Untermyer, the undisputed kingpin of Guggenheimer & Untermyer, to join him as co-counsel, representing claimants who would retain them. Born in the South in 1858, Untermyer had come to New York and established himself not only as a prominent litigator but also as a skilled negotiator of corporate mergers and reorganizations. When he died in 1940, his obituary ran on the first page of the *New York Times*—notwithstanding the war in Europe—and credited him with trying more substantial cases in court than any other member of the New York bar.

Untermyer had amassed a huge personal fortune from large fees—sometimes of a million dollars or more—in the era when the income tax was minuscule. And in those carefree days before the Securities Act and the Securities Exchange Act were passed under the Roosevelt Administration, when taking advantage of inside information was an accepted practice considered "shrewd business," he made millions more by buying and selling the stock of corporations such as Fox Films and Bethlehem Steel with whose reorganizations he was intimately involved as a lawyer.

He lived like a baron. He had a large apartment on Fifth Avenue for weekdays; a huge Yonkers estate called Greystone, the former home of Samuel J. Tilden, for weekends and springtime; a home named The Willows in Palm Springs, California, which he used from January to April, traveling to and fro in a private railroad car; and a home on Brant Lake in the Adirondacks for the summer. His greenhouses at Greystone were among the very largest in America, and during their heyday he employed sixty-two full-time gardeners. From his greenhouses came his hallmark, the fresh orchid that he wore in his buttonhole each day.

These splendid trappings of Untermyer's life were partly what made Hays select him. He felt, correctly, that showing off Untermyer to claimants would persuade them not to go elsewhere for legal representation. Furthermore, Untermyer was a great power in the New York City Bar. Hays had dealt with Untermyer both as an adversary and as co-counsel previously and was much impressed by his skill at negotiating what Hays felt would be a difficult-to-come-by but large settlement. As the case progressed, Hays would be disappointed that Untermyer's firm did not share the burden of legal work; his own would carry the bulk of it, as Untermyer, the commanding general, criticized from the sidelines. But when the settlement came, the shrewd Untermyer would more than redeem himself.

The battle lines were now to be drawn for the lawyers and Surrogate to occupy.

6.

2,303 CLAIMANTS

What a man wishes, he generally believes to be true.
DEMOSTHENES
THIRD OLYNTHIAC, 349 B.C.

A week after Ella's death, the executors Charles Koss, his daughter Isabel, and Stanley Shirk, filed her will. They petitioned the Surrogate for temporary administration to enable them to collect rents, which they estimated at $1½ million per year, and manage the Wendel real estate until the will was probated. The two New York County Surrogates alternated duties from month to month, one conducting trials and the other ruling on petitions such as these. By chance, Surrogate Foley was conducting trials in March 1931, so the petition came before Surrogate John P. O'Brien, later to be Mayor of New York City. He granted their petition and fixed a bond of

$2,635,000 to ensure the faithful performance of their duties.

The executors conceded that:

> an extensive investigation must be made to ascertain, if possible, who are the heirs and next of kin of said decedent, and due to the fact that decedent's remote ancestors were from Europe (Germany) and some in other States, delay of many months will necessarily ensue before the will can be probated.

But the petition maintained that they had "satisfied themselves that Ella had no relatives whatever."

Under probate law, heirs are entitled to contest a will if certain issues are under dispute. The grounds to contest Ella Wendel's will were the questions of her mental competence and the extent of Koss's influence. If the will was denied probate—that is, judicially determined to be invalid—and if no valid prior will satisfied the same tests, then the heirs would be entitled to divide her estate as if she had died intestate, leaving no will at all.

Before the Proponents could uphold the will, they were required to find the legitimate heirs. So Warren engaged two genealogists, Paul E. Schwabe and William A. Robbins, to make the investigation. Robbins, a member of the New York Bar, concentrated on the Dew and Stansbury relatives of Ella's mother, Mary Ann Dew the Amiable. His investigations began with the Wendel family Bible, the Bible of Rebecca Swope, and a genealogical statement in the handwriting of Ella's father, John D. Wendel. Another thread to unravel was the Astor connection of Ella's grandmother, Elizabeth, that wound through such prominent New York and British lines as the Delanos, the Stuyvesants, the Brevoorts, and the Roosevelts. Schwabe, a graduate of the University of Leipzig, Germany, conducted the search in Europe, tracing the Wendel clan from which Johann, Ella's grandfather, had departed when he came to America.

In addition Warren assigned a young office associate, Charles E. Halstead, to work on Ella's competence and her domicile, as well as to handle some troublesome claims that emerged in the South.

That fateful statement "no relatives whatever" unleashed a torrent of publicity around the world. The newspaper and wire service accounts penetrated the most remote backwaters of the United States and Europe. And once the floodgates were opened, the claims began to pour in.

Almost all the claimants were elderly and poor and could not afford a lawyer's fees, so they had to find New York attorneys who would take their cases on a contingent basis, for a percentage of the recovery. Most sought the help of their home-town lawyers in approaching New York counsel. Some read of the names of lawyers in newspaper accounts and seized on them to represent their claims.

There was a huge outpouring of persons from Europe—mainly Germany, Belgium, and Austria—who shared Ella's open-sesame, far-from-rare name. As Foley said at a hearing, "From abroad we have claims filed by whole villages whose inhabitant bear only the name of Wendel." Some families raised funds and sent delegates from Europe to establish their right to inherit and take the money home on the next boat. Others appealed to U.S. consuls in various European countries to help find American lawyers to press their claims. The government of Czechoslovakia urged its Wendel heirs to file claims through a special branch of its Foreign Office.

Among the claimants, there were 212 who had Wendel as their family or given or maiden name, 72 claimants who had Dew as one of their names, and 163 who had Stansbury. Since no one would let a misplaced vowel keep him from his rightful fortune, one Windel and four Windle claimants emerged. Nor would a dropped or added consonant prove an obstacle to entitlement—as four Wendels, nine Wendells, and three Windells affirmed.

Many claimants wrote to Koss or Warren, whose names were in all the newspapers. In an affidavit filed in court, Warren stated he had received more than twelve hundred queries. Some were as unsubstantiated as the one from a Wisconsin mailman who had suddenly grown conscious that he was "one of the Wendels," or as simple as the postcard that read:

Sirs: Maybe I am connected with the Wendels.
Truly yours,
George X. Decker

Some claims relied on family Bibles, others on family legends of rich relatives somewhere. A typical one came addressed to "The Wendel Estate":

I read a little editorial in the paper about the death of Miss Ella Wendel. My father's name is Wendel and I believe we are of some relation to Miss Ella. When Henry George died the facts they had in the paper concerning the past of himself and his family corresponded with the past and the ways in which my grandfather's folks lived. . . . Can you give me a little more information about the past and the death of Miss Ella . . .
Mrs. J. Spanjersberg

And some, like this one Koss received, adopted a more confident tone:

Will you kindly inform me of the proper procedure to put my name on file and the necessary data as an heir of the Wendel Estate.
(Mrs.) Alice Wendel Chapelle

Others decided that an appeal directly to Harlan's pocketbook offered the best hope. One Wendel in Clintonville, Wisconsin, offered to go fifty-fifty if Harlan could get him $25,000. Mrs B. P. Hull of Bedford, Virginia, wrote that she and Ella were very close friends and saw each other quite often in Summit, New Jersey, in the fall of 1929. Mrs. Hull was so pleased that Ella had left her the house at 442 Fifth Avenue; if Harlan would sell it for her, he could share equally in the proceeds.

More than two hundred attorneys would eventually be engaged to represent the 2,303 claimants. Imagine the high hopes of each of those lawyers that he had drawn the lucky claimant who was the sole heir. Most lawyers had 5 or fewer hopefuls, and some had as many as 10. Edward Friedlander, Esq., of Brooklyn had 26; Fred Boehm, Esq., of 17 John Street had 25; Boker and Epstein, Esqs., of 18 E. 41 Street had 19; Single and Hill, Esqs., of 15 William Street had 48; and T. C. Drinnan of Knoxville Tennessee, had 101. But the clear winners, in numbers of claimants, were Harry Hall, Esq., and Bernard Kovner, Esq., of 41 Park Row—representing 291. It boggles the mind to think of the Herculean efforts Hall and Kovner must have expended in keeping the records of each claimant separate.

Meantime, what was Arthur Garfield Hays up to? There had been a series of four feature articles in early April 1931, written by Forrest Davis, in the *World Telegram*, about Ella, the Wendel fortune, and her eccentric ways. Hays had read them. Toward the end of April 1931, an Indianapolis lawyer named Lawrence Shaw brought Hays his first clients. Shaw represented a group of claimants who believed themselves close relatives by descent from one Peter Wendel, who came from Germany in 1839 and settled in Chambersburg, Pennsylvania. They had selected Hays because of his national reputation and had collected a fund to retain him. Although Hays took them on, ultimately they were never able to prove that

Peter Wendel had a place on Ella's family tree. He then went to visit Forrest Davis, who was an old crony from the days of the Scopes trial, which Davis had covered. He received from Davis all of the additional information Davis had gathered and made it clear that if they would help each other, Davis would not suffer from the cooperation. Davis's stories were to mention Hays, noting his prior triumphs at the bar and his connection with the ACLU, and Untermyer, emphasizing his reputation—to imply that they were the counsel best able to represent Wendel claimants. Hays also planted in these stories that Clarence Darrow would come out of retirement to help oppose the probate of Ella's will, but Darrow was too old and sick to participate.

In a footnote to *City Lawyer*, Hays says that, at the end of the case, his firm issued to Davis a check for $5,000. Today such a payment would certainly raise eyebrows at the Ethics Committee of the Bar Association.

Who were the persons who could claim as heir in Ella's estate and challenge the probate of her will? If Ella had died a few months earlier, the legal entanglements would have been even more horrendous. Prior to December 1, 1930, New York law provided that different persons were heirs of real estate than those who were heirs of personal property such as cash, stocks, and bonds. In 1929 Governor Roosevelt of New York had appointed a Commission to Investigate Defects in the Law of Estates. The chairman, naturally, was Surrogate Foley.

The Commission report recommended that the distinction between persons inheriting real and personal property be abolished. It had been brought to America from England, originally arising from the feudal system. England had in 1925 abolished the distinction; three-fourths of the states in America had done likewise. The inheritance under then-existing New York law was thereby vastly more complicated, and to no end. In feudal days, land was the sole source of wealth. In the

United States over 90 percent of all decedents left only personal property.

Based on the committee's recommendation, the New York legislature abolished the distinction, effective December 1, 1930. So if Ella's will was denied probate, the same persons would inherit Ella's real and personal property as her closest living relatives.

But how was the degree of relationship to be determined? The rule of computation requires the exclusion of Ella. Each claimant was to count—and each count was a degree—starting with himself in the chain of ascent of his or her family tree to and including the common ancestor with Ella and then in descent counting each subsequent descendant from that common ancestor to Ella. In short, each claimant was to go up his branch of the tree and then down Ella's branch, each ancestor being a degree.

And so the claims poured into the Surrogate's Court, each affirming, but without documentary proof, relationship to Ella, the woman with "no relatives whatever."

7.

ROSA DEW STANSBURY

Sprightly, weighing 80 pounds, she remarks "Don't call me that little old woman."
NEW YORK TIMES
SEPTEMBER 28, 1931

If there were no shortages of Wendels in Germany, there was a surfeit of Dews and Stansburys in America. During his ninety-two years, General Stansbury had married three wives; the first bore four children, the second four more. And Mary Ann Dew the Amiable, his granddaughter and Ella's mother, had four brothers and a sister.

The Proponents had not been sleeping on these leads. As Warren stated in an affidavit, his researchers had

> examined records in the states of Maryland, Pennsylvania, Missouri, Ohio, New York, in the District of Columbia and in Germany. In these places they have examined records of wills and the probate thereof, administrations, guardianships, land records, court records, church records, tombstones in cemeteries

> and they have interviewed many persons and examined documents in the possession of many persons bearing the family name of the decedent or of any of her ancestors or claiming to be descended from ancestors of the decedent. They have also examined records in the various historical and genealogical societies, files of newspapers published in various cities and records of vital statistics in most of the states mentioned in Germany; they have also examined census records, records in the Congressional Library and records of vital statistics in Washington, D.C.

As a result of these efforts, Warren's affidavit concluded, "I believe . . . that Rosa Dew Stansbury is the only heir, next of kin and distributee."

Certainly Rosa Dew Stansbury—a first-cousin once removed, with a fifth-degree relationship to Ella Wendel—was the closest proven heir to surface so far.

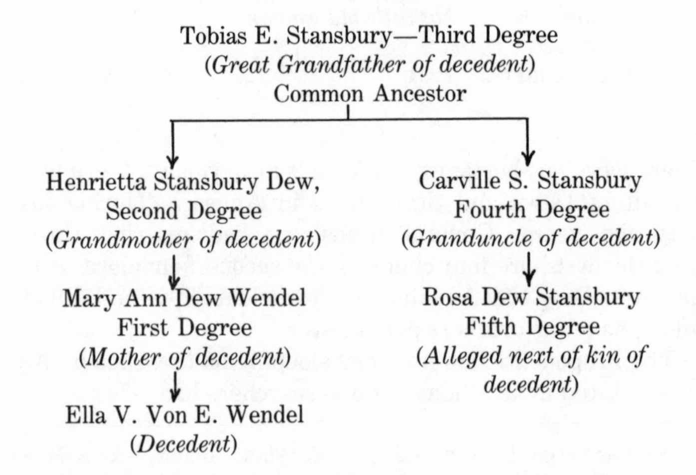

Warren invited Rosa to New York City, and she accepted, although her lawyer, Winfield P. Jones, of Atlanta, was on vacation. Accompanied by her nephew, M.C. Childs, she met with Warren and—without advice of counsel—signed a waiver of citation and consent to probate, dated August 31, 1931. In exchange she received $1,000 down and a promise of $24,000 more if she proved to be the sole heir and if the will was admitted to probate. Rosa claimed she had told Warren that Jones would have to approve the agreement when he returned from vacation, but Warren denied that she had made any such proviso.

It was an instant sensation in the newspapers. Rosa made extremely good copy. A seventy-four-year-old spinster, less than five feet tall, she had a Cinderella background, being forced by straitened circumstances to become a paid companion to Mrs. Alice Calder of New Orleans. Reporters found her bubbly and full of life, excited at being interviewed for the first time in her life. She had no idea what she would do with the Wendel fortune and only wished she were younger to enjoy it longer.

In a textbook illustration of the maxim that a client should be forbidden to talk to the press—especially without her lawyer present—Rosa concluded the interview:

> She did not want "anyone" to say anything "bad" about Miss Wendel, and admitted that she did not like to hear of anyone challenging the recluse's "testamentary." She indicated, quite clearly, that she would rather lose the fortune than obtain it at the cost of showing Miss Wendel was incapable of making a will.

These were not her lawyer's sentiments by a long shot. Presumably after a stern admonition, in more Southern gentlemanly language, to keep her mouth shut, she never repeated them.

Hays read these newspaper accounts with consternation. He had a retainer agreement with Nannie F. Gollrick of Baltimore, a probably sixth-degree claimant, and others from assorted Dews and Stansburys. As he described in his book, almost every day ancient jalopies would pull up in front of his office at 43 Exchange Place. Out would come the bearers of photos of tombstones, of moldering family Bibles, of yellowing church records, of certificates of birth and marriage, and of pedigree declarations by people in their eighties that—yes, indeed—each claimant was the sole Wendel heir. Since many of these claimants were quite advanced in years, how could Rosa, from the generation before them, still be alive? She would have to be a hundred years old.

Hays invited Jones to come from Atlanta, and he arrived with Childs and John Grant, another of Rosa's nephews. Hays decided to "Untermyer" the Southerners. Escorting them to Greystone in Yonkers, he showed them around the large mansion, the extensive greenhouses, and the spacious grounds. In these surroundings, Rosa's settlement of $25,000 shrank and shrank. Untermyer outlined his approach to the problem, and his listeners became more and more confident. Hays says Untermyer never had doubt about any case he handled—and that his clients, after being exposed to him, never had any, either.

As Rosa's attorney, Jones retained Hays-Untermyer and returned the $1,000 to Warren. Untermyer then wrote to Warren, declaring that he considered the waiver of citation void. He invited Warren to his office to discuss the matter, but Warren ignored the offer. So Hays then made a statement to the press:

> We are not troubled by an agreement made by a woman more than seventy-four years of age, without the advice of counsel and without full knowledge of the facts that should have been revealed to her. The agreement itself is so unconscionable that we cannot conceive of its recognition by any court. Why, she signed a release for an amount that was less than the interest on the estate for a single half-hour.

And Childs, who had been present when Rosa signed, added that he had been

> informed by George Flint Warren . . . that Miss Stansbury had no rights whatever, that "consent to probate would avoid publicity" and that they were giving her the $25,000 as a matter of charity to the nearest relative of the deceased.

The mystery of how Rosa was only seventy-four was quickly explained, by the unusual marriage of her mother, Harriet Louisa Stansbury. According to a contemporary account:

> Harriet Louisa was the youngest of thirteen children. Upon the death of her parents she and some of the other children came back to Baltimore from Louisiana, to live with their grandfather, Gen. Stansbury. After his death they continued to live at the old home place. The elder children, or some of them, tried to promote a marriage for Harriet with a wealthy old gentleman of the neighborhood.
>
> Meanwhile she had become infatuated with her uncle, and one day she rode into Baltimore attired in a green velvet riding habit and they were quietly married without the knowledge of her sisters and brothers. The marriage was kept a secret for a few months.

In fact, Carville Stansbury, her husband, was her half-uncle, a son of her grandfather by a different grandmother. But the marriage was possibly invalid under Maryland law as incestuous, since Harriet was half of the same blood as Carville. If it prove invalid, would Rosa be disqualified from inheriting? The Hays office researched and prepared an elaborate memorandum of law; a similar thought had occurred to Root Clark, and their files contained an equally elaborate memorandum of law.

The reader who is exposed weekly to newspaper articles containing charges of "conflict of interest" against lawyers and business men may be wondering how Hays and Untermyer avoided this charge. It was clear that only the persons in the closest degree to Ella would be entitled to challenge probate or to receive a financial settlement for forgoing that challenge.

Before Rosa switched attorneys, Hays-Untermyer had thirty clients claiming sixth-degree relationship to Ella, twenty-four clients claiming seventh-degree, and eleven clients claiming eighth-degree. How could Hays-Untermyer take on Rosa, an undisputed fifth-degree claimant, when she would eliminate their other clients? Wouldn't their representing her constitute a conflict of interest?

When asked about this, Judge Friendly recalled that he had wondered himself at the time. Hays had, as he saw it, made it a race-track parimutuel, where everyone got something for running; the winner got the most, and the second, third, and later finishers got proportionately less. In *City Lawyer* Hays calls the arrangement a "pooling agreement." Each party entering contributed to the disbursement fund to be expended to win the contest. Only those whose relationship was "established" would share in the recovery.

The legal battle would now begin in earnest.

8.

PRELIMINARY LEGAL SKIRMISHING

This must not drift into a farce or reproach to our probate system. . . . I will not permit it to drag out and become a subject of ridicule. . . . I think the question of the [Surrogate] Court's jurisdiction [New York or Westchester] should forever be quieted. Most of the estate consists of real estate, and if the case is kept open for 100 years we will never be able to effect a proper conveyance of it."

SURROGATE FOLEY
MARCH 21, 1932

With Rosa Dew Stansbury as a client, Hays-Untermyer in September 1931 filed a bill of complaint in the Federal Court of the Southern District, New York. They sought a temporary injunction to prevent the Proponents from using Rosa's consent to probate, which they alleged was procured by fraud and overreaching, as a basis for probating Ella's will. Since Rosa was from Mississippi and the Proponents were New York residents, the Federal court, based upon diversity of citizenship would have jurisdiction over the question. At the same time, Judge Julian W. Mack issued a temporary restraining order of the probate proceedings until the case was argued before him.

At this point, Warren and the attorneys for the Residuary Charities engaged Root Clark as counsel. Root Clark cross-moved to dismiss the complaint so that the New York probate proceeding, commenced three days earlier, could continue.

The hearing in Judge Mack's chambers was set for late October 1931, to enable both parties to submit extensive memoranda of law and elaborate affidavits. The brief was written largely by Friendly, who was considered an expert on federal jurisdiction questions by virtue of his service with Justice Brandeis and his studies with Professor Felix Frankfurter. Hays and Untermyer argued for Rosa, and Buckner for the Proponents.

In an article written later for the *Harvard Law Review*, honoring Justice Harlan, Judge Friendly called the outcome of that hearing one of the first applications of Federal judicial abstention. Judge Mack ruled that while the Federal court had jurisdiction, it should abstain from taking the case, on the ground that the issues—whether Rosa was entitled to contest the probate of Ella's will and whether her waiver was valid—were so intimately connected with the probate itself that the Surrogate's Court should decide them as well. Both sides were reasonably content with the decision. Harlan in the Root Clark *Bull* called it "a complete victory for us"; Hays in his book said, "The proceeding gave us a breathing space and relieved our anxiety that there would be an immediate probate of the will."

With the jurisdiction matter resolved, the scene now shifts across Centre Street near City Hall to the Surrogate's Court. The court is housed in a turn-of-the-century building now designated a national historical landmark. Its thick walls are paneled with beautifully carved wood, its doors graced with elegant wooden swags; in the days before amplification, its lofty ceilings made for terrible acoustics. Room 503, where the case would be heard, might have been styled for a Venetian doge; at its rear, stairs climb to a minstrel gallery overlooking the courtroom. It was Foley's courtroom, and there his portrait in oils hangs today.

Meantime, behind the scenes at the Surrogate's Court there was some pushing and shoving going on between Foley and O'Brien as to who would handle the Wendel estate. It had come to O'Brien by chance. But Foley felt entitled to it by virtue of seniority and also—however tactfully he phrased it to O'Brien—by virtue of his considerably greater intellect and learning. Whichever argument he used, Foley won.

So O'Brien's last connection with the Wendel estate came when Hays-Untermyer moved before Surrogate O'Brien to revoke the letters of administration issued to Koss, his daughter, and Stanley Shirk—their ground being that Ella was a resident of Westchester. Root Clark opposed. O'Brien invoked "sound and sensible procedure" to rule that the issue of residence be tried before Surrogate Foley, and then he disappeared from the Wendel Estate.

Like ordinary men, Surrogates enjoy favorable publicity, which was in no short supply in the Wendel matter. Then, too, Foley must have been intrigued by the challenges of managing a case, with its extraordinary number of claimants and a host of complications, and disposing of it properly and expeditiously. In its magnitude it was the equivalent of singlehandedly building a bridge or digging a tunnel.

Meantime, Root Clark had moved into high gear. The first problem was the claims, then numbering over sixteen hundred, most without merit. With very rare exceptions, the claimants had not submitted documentary proof of relationship to Ella—a clear imperative. To simplify the process,

Friendly drafted a form of Bill of Particulars for each claimant to verify under oath and then file in court. As an illustration, its first page set forth particulars of Rosa Dew Stansbury's lineage; the second page had a blank family tree for the claimant. After Harlan revised Friendly's draft, Foley made further amendments. Root Clark then formally applied to the Surrogate for an order that each claimant prepare and file such a Bill. Their application was opposed by a dozen lawyers, who feared it would expose the weakness of their clients' claims.

The *New York Times* reported that pandemonium reigned in the usually staid courtroom, with 160 lawyers and as many claimants clamoring to offer suggestions on the conduct of the case. The Surrogate was irked at the babble and confusion and made his displeasure obvious. He reserved decision on how he would simplify the tangled issues.

Two weeks later, Foley issued an opinion that:

1. The first issue to be tried and determined was whether Ella was domiciled in Westchester of New York; for, if the former, the entire case would be transferred up there.
2. If New York had jurisdiction, then the court would determine the relationship of the claimants to Ella, beginning with those claiming the nearest degree. Once the nearest degree claimant(s) had been established, all claims of more remote relatives would be struck out, on motion of the Proponents.
3. If Rosa proved to be of the nearest degree, the validity of her waiver of citation and consent to probate would be tried.
4. Finally, if there were heirs (Rosa or others) legally entitled to contest the will, that issue would then be tried.

He granted the Proponents' application, ordered them to print a supply, and required each claimant to file a verified Bill of Particulars. And he adopted a suggestion made at the hearing that the Proponents prepare a chart of the Wendel family tree from Ella's eight great-grandparents downward. The four- by six-foot diagram, secured to roller rods like a classroom map, was later hung in the probate department of the court. It would be revised more than once as the case progressed.

Then he fixed a time for trying Ella's domicile—early May 1932.

9.

WHERE WAS ELLA'S DOMICILE?

It was natural that she [Ella] should return [from Westchester in February 1929] to a domicile at her home in the city [New York] and county where the family fortune was accumulated and the great bulk of her properties located.

DECISION OF SURROGATE FOLEY
JUNE 18, 1932

After Ella died, George Flint Warren filed her will and codicils in—and received letters of temporary administration from—the Surrogate's Court of New York County. Obviously he could have had no warning of the contest that would develop over her domicile. Yet he ignored Ella's solemn (if anything Ella ever did could be called solemn) statement in her final codicil, executed twenty-one months before her death, that she was "of Irvington, Westchester County." No one ever questioned Warren on why he did this. A shrewd guess might be that he did it purely for his own convenience. The New York Surrogate's Court was an eight-block walk from his office, while the Westchester County Surrogate's Court in White Plains was an hour and a half away by the subway and train.

But, granting this, why were Hays-Untermyer so determined to take the estate to Westchester, and why was Root Clark equally firm on keeping it in New York? The reasons, like everything else in the case, were far from straightforward. Some rested more on emotion than on rational judgment. Others were frankly contradictory.

For one thing, Foley was the son-in-law of Charlie Murphy, the Head of Tammany Hall, who ran New York County as a personal Democratic party fiefdom. It was no coincidence that Foley became a Surrogate in 1920 at the unusually young age of thirty-eight. Furthermore, Tammany Hall had elected Foley its head in 1924, after Murphy let go of the reins. Foley declined the honor, but it was not forgotten at the bar. No hint of scandal ever touched Foley in his twenty-five years on the bench, but often senior lawyers preferred to avoid him when facing strong Democratic adversaries.

In 1931 Root Clark had no political ties to the Democratic Party, and for that matter neither had Hays. But Untermyer was extremely well connected in Democratic circles. It would seem that he would want Foley to preside over the case. The Westchester Surrogate, George A. Slater, was a capable, honorable man but fell far short of Foley in intellect and in knowledge of estate law.

During the preliminary maneuvering over Ella's domicile, Untermyer stayed at his home in Palm Springs. From there he could command and castigate Hays, while remaining aloof from the proceedings. At one point, he commented to his nephew and junior partner, Lawrence A. Steinhardt (later

Roosevelt's Ambassador to Sweden, Russia, and Turkey), for transmission to Hays:

> In my judgment, in the present proceeding we will be, and deserve to be, unmercifully beaten. If the papers had been sent me, and a detailed outline of what was intended to be done, I would have tried to stop it.

His overall instruction to Hays was:

> I consider it of the utmost importance to get away from the Surrogate's Court, New York County. We should be preparing our papers to that end, having in mind that we shall get no relief until we reach the Appellate Courts.

In his book Hays says that removal to Westchester would mean the estate would pass to "other and more neutral hands"—although Foley had shown no bias on the two largest issues, Rosa's waiver of citation and Ella's competence to make a valid will. However, he had wrested the case from Surrogate O'Brien, and this fact was not lost on Untermyer. Ultimately, Will Maslow remembers, Untermyer wanted Slater because his adversaries wanted Foley so badly—not an uncommon or foolish influence on lawyers' thinking.

Furthermore, Hays-Untermyer had demanded a jury trial on the issue of whether the will should be probated. Untermyer felt a Westchester jury verdict on Ella's capacity to make a will would favor the claimants. Judge Friendly recalls that, at the time, Root Clark took the opposite view. The Proponents felt that a jury drawn from Ella's country neighbors would be sympathetic to her simple ways and idiosyncrasies; a tougher, more cynical New York City jury, jealous of her enormous fortune, would regard her mental competence and Koss's alleged undue influence far less favorably. But on balance Root Clark preferred Foley, based on its study of his past performance in will probate contests. A tough and confident Surrogate, Foley was not easily fooled; he was known for taking cases away from the jury and deciding them himself as a matter of law—almost always on the side of admitting the will to probate.

For some months now, the rival sides had been gathering ammunition on the twin issues of Ella's domicile and competence. Hays had dispatched Will Maslow to Irvington, where he bought a barrel of Ella Wendel letters and talked to former servants, tradesmen, bank officers, neighbors, local ministers, and others. He also examined Westchester court records on Ella's deceased siblings and deeds and other papers Ella had signed. Back in New York City, he interviewed Ella's past and recent servants at 442, as well as her other contacts. Much of what is known today about Ella's curious life comes from Maslow's memorandum to Hays.

With its greater staff and greater financial resources, Root Clark did prodigious research under Harlan's generalship. In a memorandum to the Residuary Charities, preliminary to discussing Root Clark's fees, Buckner stated that his researchers had interviewed more than a hundred people. Alphonse Laporte and Wallace Bates, of Root Clark's Washington office, combed census records back to 1860 for all Wendel family members; their task was complicated by the fact that 442 Fifth Avenue had at some uncertain time been known as 396 Fifth. Error had to be sorted from truth, as when Rebecca's census form for 1920 claimed Irish parentage on both sides. Harlan's instructions, when the census records were located, were that they be then certified with "lots of seals" for use at the hearing.

His staff searched the State Department for Wendel passport applications, from the present to the time of the Civil War. They dug through voter lists in Albany for Irvington and

New York City, as far back as the 1870s. Harlan had one associate scour all New York City directories from the earliest date; another inspect residence statements made in records of interment in the Wendel vault in Trinity Church, as well as all Wendel death and baptismal certificates; and still others search for pew rentals in various churches, and tabulate residences stated in powers of attorney and other family documents. All old wills, probate papers, and Federal tax returns were unearthed and studied for residence statements, as were old leases Ella had signed. Young attorney Robert D. Fiske, who would later become an important executive of American Cyanamid Corporation, reviewed the records in sixteen different banks, looking for residence statements. All former Wendel servants were interviewed, including one, Minnie Lee, then eighty-one years old, who had worked for the Wendels in the 1870s; and Schwabe was even sent to talk to ex-employees retired in Schleswig-Holstein.

MacLean and Jack Merrill, now a retired senior partner of Emmet, Marvin & Martin, searched file cabinets in Quogue and Irvington for other proofs of domicile.

MacLean recalls a humorous episode that occurred during this tedious process. One of the Root Clark associates found an old piece of paper and, imitating Ella's childish scrawl, composed a note to Beckie: "I am looking forward to being at our own dear home at 442 Fifth for Christmas." Enclosing it in an old envelope, he slipped it on the desk of another associate who was reading mountains of letters. Finally his colleague found it, and with a great shout of joy, rushed into the hall to announce his discovery—where the peals of laughter greeting him revealed the practical joke.

By then Buckner had suffered a stroke, and Elihu Root, Jr., was brought in to help Harlan, if needed. It was MacLean who prepared the exhaustive memorandum of the law of domicile that Friendly used, together with various memos on the evidence, in writing the trial brief to be submitted to Foley. The major thrust of the brief was that Ella, as a child, had the domicile of her parents—clearly 442 Fifth. If during her lifetime Ella did not change her domicile to Irvington—there was much conflicting evidence on his point—then she was still domiciled in New York. Thus, Root Clark placed the burden of proving change of domicile on Hays and Untermyer.

The hearing before Foley on May 4, 1932, was tried by Harlan (with Root, Friendly, Warren, and Hewitt of counsel) for the Proponents and by Hays and Untermyer (with John Schulman, Raymond St. John, and others of counsel) for Rosa Dew Stansbury. Many of the other claimants and their attorneys were present, but didn't participate.

Harlan opened by introducing as exhibits various family documents, yellowed with age, showing that all the Wendels had considered 442 Fifth their domicile. "We have no birth record or baptismal record of Ella," he continued, and then proceeded to read the entry of her birth from the family Bible. Next he presented the will of Ella's father, John D., who called 442 "my dwelling" and described the Irvington estate variously as "my country house," "my farm," and "my country seat."

At this point, the first witness, Koss, was helped to the stand by a court attendant. Koss testified that he first became acquainted with the Wendel family around 1867. He stated that he had witnessed John D.'s will and confirmed that, indeed, the will (from the days before typewriters) was written in Koss's own handwriting. When Harlan handed him the will, Koss was deeply affected at the sight of the document. His face started to twitch and his hands began to shake. He took a pill but appeared to grow weaker and was unable to speak. Foley then adjourned the hearing to allow Koss to go home.

Morris Shilensky, then an office boy in the Hays office, vividly remembers Untermyer's response. Then seventy-four years old, Untermyer was not in the best of health. Foley had given him permission to remain seated while addressing the court, instead of rising as other lawyers did. But now Untermyer rose to his feet. In a "quavering voice," he urged the court to perpetuate Koss's testimony by going to his residence, because of the "uncertainties of life." Foley acceded to the request, and the next day Foley, the court stenographer, and all the lawyers convened at Koss's West End Avenue home.

At the subsequent session, Shirk testified for the Proponents that all the Wendel family heirlooms, the family Bible, their family pictures, their library, and their statuary were kept at 442. He vividly described the mansion, with its lack of steam heat or electricity, its zinc bathtub, and details of its 1850s decor. The eight safes at 442 contained all the abstracts and deeds of their real estate holdings. In New York, Ella had eight bank accounts, totaling nearly $5 million, but the Tarrytown account used for the Irvington property had only $9,000. Untermyer countered, on cross-examination, by introducing into evidence an undated letter from Ella, undoubtedly copied from a letter prepared by Koss, to the United States Trust Company. In it she stated that, with regard to her Federal, State, and City income taxes, "I now reside in Irvington."

Then came William Diaz, of the Wendel office, who described himself as secretary to the family. He too noted the lack of modern comforts at both 442 and Irvington, but added that at 442 the old ways had been preserved as a kind of memorial to Ella's parents. Isabel Koss Murray (she had married since Ella's death) testified there was nothing at 442 that hadn't been there for many years, except for a pair of scissors she had bought. And Annie Gavin, Ella's personal maid for twenty years, offered that it was only the coal soot in New

York City, which soiled Tobey's coat, that drove Ella to Irvington; she scored for the Proponents by testifying that Ella's trunks were inscribed *EVW, N.Y.*

The claimants brought various witnesses to attest to Ella's domicile in Westchester, but these provided nothing noteworthy or conclusive. Finally, all arguments had been presented. After complimenting the attorneys on their exhaustive preparation and clear presentation of the voluminous evidence, Foley reserved his decision to give both sides the chance to submit briefs.

Elihu Root, Jr., writing in the *Bull*, said:

> The writer was supposed to be responsible for arguments on points of evidence, but as the Surrogate knew the law and ruled favorably on all of the substantial points without waiting for argument, that duty was not an onerous one. . . . I want to say personally that John Harlan did a swell job as trial counsel. He was far more effective than his redoubtable antagonist [Untermyer], better grounded in his case, clearer in his examinations, and far superior in his knowledge of the law.

Foley's opinion of June 16, 1932, did not surprise either side. He did not buy the Root Clark argument that Ella's domicile remained the same as her parents' until her death—that argument might have validity if Ella had died as a girl of twenty-one. But in seventy-eight years, surely Ella had the right to, and in fact had, established her own domicile.

Foley decided that:

> 1. From her birth in 1853 until about 1881, Ella was domiciled in New York.
>
> 2. From 1881 to 1926, she clearly had abandoned her New York domicile and established her domicile in Irvington.

3. In the transitional period from 1926 to 1929, Ella made conflicting declarations as to her domicile.

4. From 1929 to the date of her death, her written declarations "with few exceptions" stated that she resided in New York.

And then, as his clinching argument, Foley ruled that Ella's domicile was where her great fortune was located—New York City. Thus, pulling himself up by his own bootstraps, with brute force, Foley was able to decide, to his own satisfaction, that he could keep control of the case.

For the conflicting documentary evidence, excluding wills and codicils, really proved nothing—Diaz, Shirk, Koss, and Warren were not focused on this issue when they prepared various papers that Ella signed without reading. If she was in residence at 442 Fifth, the papers stated that as her residence; if at Irvington (as she was eight or nine months each year), and the paper had to be taken up to have her sign and a Westchester notary public attest her signature, the papers stated that to be her residence. The only cardinal principle, as Rabell, who succeeded Koss as John G.'s lawyer, testified, was that wherever New York City taxes were involved, Ella definitely became a Westchester resident.

In fact, Foley's rationale for his decision—that Ella lived where her great fortune was located—was ludicrous. She neither had knowledge of nor cared a damn for her fortune. She was only interested in haggling over a dollar per week less on a servant's wages or the size of the tradesmen's bills. She didn't install a furnace in Irvington because she couldn't afford it. Charles Ahrens, the Wendel carpenter, told Maslow that when Ella's lawyers told her that they had obtained a $40,000 tax refund, Ella replied, "I have no time to bother with such things. I am too busy with my own affairs." And Rose Camp, Ella's laundress, quoted her to Maslow as saying, "I do not care what becomes of the money after I am gone. Let them throw it away or do whatever they want with it."

Ella's business affairs were handled by Koss or the Wendel family office. The best expression of Ella's own position was probably her complaint to Geisse, a friend, that they kept bringing her stacks of papers to sign "which I cannot understand and am not interested in."

Will Maslow remembers being very unhappy with the decision, which he considered motivated by Foley's desire to keep the case in order to dispense patronage. He felt that it tarnished Foley's extraordinary and well-deserved reputation. Hays and Untermyer, of course, were extremely displeased and immediately filed an appeal. Briefs for the appeal were prepared by both sides.

10.

NEW FIFTH-DEGREE CLAIMANTS SURFACE

I can imagine some reader saying, "It is surprising Hays is so frank about all this. Weren't he and Untermyer engaged in high-class 'ambulance chasing'!" Not at all!

HAYS
CITY LAWYER

Hays was not satisfied that he had the winner in the Wendel sweepstakes. There might be a fourth-degree claimant, someone more closely related to Ella than Rosa Dew Stansbury. Because of his "pooling agreement," Hays felt that he had better search and find such a claimant, if he or she existed.

James Cromwell Dew, Ella's maternal grandfather, had married twice. From his first marriage, the only child was the amiable Mary Ann Dew. With his second wife, Ann Barney Williams, from a prominent Baltimore family, he had five more children: Rebecca, John Hammond, Thomas, Nicholson, and George Stiles Dew. Rebecca and Nicholson died in infancy, but the three remaining brothers survived to adulthood.

The family legend had it that John Hammond Dew, born in 1813, had shipped out to Australia as a young man. There he may have established a tavern in some unknown city—but then, perhaps he hadn't—and was never heard from again. Through the good offices of Forrest Davis, Hays sent up a trial-balloon story that "attorneys and investigators" were combing Australia to find John Hammond Dew's descendants. If these searchers were apocryphal, the Australian claimants were not. They poured out of the outback in such numbers that the Australian consul general begged Hays for help in replying to their claim letters.

And then a startling piece of news emerged. On the Proponents' side, Robbins and Strube had been investigating the James Cromwell Dew family tree as well. They had satisfied themselves that neither John Hammond Dew nor Thomas Dew, Mary Ann's half-brothers, had produced any children, but that left George Stiles Dew. This remaining half-brother was born in 1822, the year his father died, and he was mentioned in his father's will. In his book, Hays claims credit for searching the acts of the Maryland legislature to find George Stiles Dew, but Will Maslow recalls he never did that research and Hays never hired a genealogist. In fact, it was Robbins and Strube who found the act of the 1825 Maryland Legislature changing George Stiles Dew's name to John Holland Barney, the name of his maternal grandfather, who adopted him as a son. But somehow the news reached Hays.

What had happened to that infant, John Holland Barney,

Jr? Hays had Forrest Davis send up a second trial balloon. The news story, naming Hays as its source, said that George Stiles Dew "went out to Missouri from Baltimore before the Civil War, got into trouble, changed his name to Barney, and emigrated to Canada." It would later be discovered that Barney had never gone to Missouri, much less to Canada, but the story would bring a number of Canadian Barneys into the estate as claimants.

Following up the Barney lead, Hays did have some investigation performed. A death notice, from January 26, 1889, in the *Baltimore Sun*, was unearthed:

> John Holland Barney, aged 67 years of Stockton, California, died yesterday. . . . In Stockton he was well known as a grain dealer but had recently retired from business. A wife, three sons and a daughter survive him.

Meanwhile, the Proponents had followed the trail through the usual genealogical searches in city directories, old newspaper files, tombstones, birth records, and the like. So by the time Hays had discovered Barney's descendants—also fifth-degree relatives of Ella—the Proponents had beaten him to it. Ben Matthews, a member of the committee of lawyers for the Residuary Charities, was already talking to attorneys for the brand-new claimants, who were seven in number, living in San Francisco, Seattle, and Spokane.

The seven claimants were represented by two lawyers, Hugh Fullerton of San Francisco and Charles P. Moriarty of Spokane. Matthews was offering cash to the Barney claimants who would assign their claims to the Residuary Charities, but both attorneys declined to commit their clients. They wanted time to size up the situation and to try to persuade Matthews to raise the ante. And then an eighth claimant surfaced—Laura Oral Harrison, who had died shortly after Ella.

Hays, of course, had hurried out to the coast to persuade the new claimants to join his team in contesting the will. He could not offer cash but did stress the huge fortune they would share. Thanks to his newspaper publicity in Los Angeles, the children of Laura contacted him, through a local lawyer, and signed retainer agreements. Meanwhile, Hays decided to woo Moriarty. He brought the attorney to New York where the Hays partners wined, dined, and theatered him. And Hays, naturally, "Untermyered" him at Greystone.

But Matthews hadn't surrendered. He and Warren continued to pursue Moriarty, assuring him that the Hays-Untermyer case was hopeless and would take many years of litigation to conclude. They also told him there were one third-degree claimant and three fourth-degree. If any of them prevailed, all fifth-degree claims were down the drain.

Finally, the five Moriarty clients decided to sell their claims to the Residuary Charities for $25,000 each—$7,500 in cash and an additional $17,500 when Ella's will was probated. In 1932, this was a princely sum to people of modest circumstances. As Moriarty described it to reporters, it was "like picking money off a manure pile." One of the five, Holland Vaughn Barney, insisted his whereabouts be concealed from the other Barneys and from his estranged wife.

Hays-Untermyer wound up with three new clients to join Rosa Dew Stansbury as fifth-degree claimants. They were Mrs. Grace Macquarrie of San Francisco, Mrs. Hattie Barney Simmons of Spokane, and the Estate of Laura Oral Harrison.

11. THOMAS PATRICK MORRIS, "SON" OF JOHN G. WENDEL, APPEARS

He told me to call him "Papa Wendel." He called me "Son."
TESTIMONY OF THOMAS PATRICK MORRIS

On May 12, 1931, two months after Ella's death, Hewitt came into Koss's office with a surprising message—a man was wait-

Thomas Patrick Morris

ing outside who claimed to be the son of John G. The two lawyers went to the reception room, where they found a balding lean man in his early fifties, dressed in neat but worn workclothes, with a smooth-shaven face and with glasses hooked over his large ears. He introduced himself as Thomas Patrick Morris, and once seated in Koss's office, related an amazing tale.

He produced a blue, clothbound book from the waistband of his pants—this was no small feat because it measured 8 by 5½ inches in size and was 1½ inches thick; it weighed more than a pound. Titled *The Blockade of Phalsburg*, it was written by Beckmann and Chatrian and published by Charles Scribners in 1900. He claimed John G. had presented the book to him in Dundee, Scotland, in 1901. Inside the front cover and continuing on the flyleaf was a letter, dated March of that year:

My dear son,

I am writing you this to clear any doubt you might have in your mind as to your parentage.

I, John G. Wendel, of 442 Fifth Avenue, New York City, and Mary Ellen Devine of Edinburgh, Scotland, were married at Castle Garden, June 11, 1876, promising to marry her later in the Church of her family, Roman Catholic. My family being Methodist, I refused to carry it through, the death of your Grandfather straightening out matters, and in the latter part of May 1879, your mother and I quarreled, and being with child she fled to friends, a Mr. and Mrs. Morris, living at 4 John Street, Dundee, Scotland. I followed and tried to make a reconciliation, but allowed religious scruples to stand in the way. You were born the 3rd of January, 1880. Your mother still refusing to be reconciled, about two weeks after your birth disappeared leaving you in bed, while our friend was out shopping. Fearing the scandal and that the news might drift back to my family in the States I failed to report it. I arranged with our friends to register your birth as their own, and care for you, living in hopes your mother would return. My hopes were in vain. You were registered as Thomas Patrick Morris, the first two names the wish of your mother, whom I dearly loved. The foregoing statement is true, So help me God.

Your loving Father,
John G. Wendel

An equally unusual document appeared inside the back cover.

I, John G. Wendel of the City of New York, County of Kings and State of New York, Do declare that owing to my sisters, especially Mary and Ella's objection and refusal to recognize my son by a secret marriage, and their threats to publicly expose me and fearing the destruction of my Will, I take this unique way to safeguard same and my son's interest. I hereby make, publish and declare, this to be my last Will, hereby revoking all former Wills made by me.

1) I direct that all my just debts be paid.

2) All my Estate, Real, Personal and mixed of whatsoever kind and wheresoever situated, I give, devise and bequeath to my son, Thomas Patrick Morris Wendel.

3) I request Charles G. Koss, our family lawyer, to be my son's adviser, in the management of the Estate. I nominate and appoint my son, Thomas Patrick Morris Wendel, as Executor of this my last Will and direct that no Bond be requested of him as such Executor.

In witness whereof I have hereunto set my hand and seal this 1st day of March 1901

(Signed) John G. Wendel
442 Fifth Ave.
New York

Witnessed by Michael Lynch,
442 Fifth Ave.,
N.Y. City

Charles Dietoch,
Libby Hotel,
N.Y. City

Richard Lundy,
442 Fifth Ave.,
N.Y. City

Koss immediately told Morris that the handwriting was not John G.'s, showing him specimens to prove it. After hesitating and saying he wasn't an expert, Morris reluctantly admitted the handwritings were not similar. Koss also mentioned that Morris did not resemble the Wendels, and, when Morris asked what he should do, advised him to retain counsel.

After ten days or so, Morris came back and asked to borrow specimans of John G.'s writing so he could get the opinion of a handwriting expert. Koss refused. He would later testify that he thought Morris was a blackmailer.

On May 20, after finding the address in the newspaper stories about Ella's estate, Morris came to Untermyer's office. There, Steinhardt, Untermyer's partner, listened to Morris's story, saw *Blockade*, and read the two documents. He then sent him to see Hays, with a memo noting that the ink in the two documents looked very new, considering its supposed thirty-year age.

Hays in turn passed Morris on to Maslow, to ascertain all the facts. Morris told him of "Papa Wendel's" visits, every two years or so, and of the presentation of the book shortly after Morris turned twenty-one. John G., he said, had cautioned him to guard the book carefully, as it would bring him great wealth someday, but to keep the gift a secret. John G. had also said that if he was ever in trouble he was to consult Koss, the family attorney.

Maslow quizzed him at length about his early life, about the visits of John G. during his infancy, and about his foster parents, Peter and Margaret Morris, and his foster brother and sisters. Morris added that, along with *Blockade*, John G. had given him a monogrammed watch and chain. He told Maslow about coming to America, meeting John G. by chance in City Hall Park, visiting 442 Fifth and there meeting Ella. From there Morris went to Arizona to work and had another chance encounter with John G. He hadn't known that John G. had died in 1914, and it was again by chance that he learned about Ella's death. So he got *Blockade* out of his trunk and went to see Koss. Eventually Hays had Morris sign an agreement retaining Hays-Untermyer to represent him.

But he continued to have Maslow investigate. From the barrel of old letters he had bought in Irvington, Maslow had specimens of John G.'s handwriting. Hays sent them, along with the book, to handwriting expert Albert D. Osborne. The report came back that the letter and "will" had not been written by John G. Still, they showed a familiarity with Wendel family affairs, and two of the witnesses to the will, Michael Lynch and Richard Lundy, were Wendel family servants; their signatures, at least to Hays's inexpert eyes, appeared to be authentic. Could John G. have procured "some confidential man" to write the documents so Thomas Patrick could not use them for blackmail?

Hays sent Maslow to do more checking. The first stop was Scribners, to see if Morris had bought the book, but since he had no picture of Morris, the trip proved fruitless. Morris had given Maslow the name of his foster sister, Rose Morris McAvan, and her husband James, so Maslow could write to them for documents bearing on the claim. Two months later, Morris finally produced their address in Dundee, Scotland, and Maslow promptly wrote to them.

In reply, Mrs. McAvan wrote Maslow that her mother, Margaret Morris, on her deathbed in 1904 had declared to her and her husband, James, that Thomas was "not my son, but the son of Mary Ellen Devine and John G. Wendel." Mr. and Mrs. McAvan "thought her delirious," and never told Thomas Patrick about the deathbed declaration.

Then—in the sort of "miracle" that regularly seemed to bless the various claimants of Ella's estate—while Rose was sorting the junk in a box under her late mother's bed, her toddler daughter playing on the floor had picked up an envelope from the pile and thereby called James's attention to it. He couldn't read but Rose could. Lo and behold, a smudged and dirty letter, dated April 6, 1897, addressed to her mother emerged:

> *My dear friend,*
>
> *I will be in Scotland for a visit some time during the month of May or June. I only wish I could get matters straightened out here with my sisters. They are hard to reason with.*
>
> *Hoping you have received my last remittance and that son Thomas P. is behaving himself, I will close with best regards and fine health.*
>
> *I remain your sincere friend,*
>
> *John G. Wendel*
> *175 Broadway*
> *New York City*

Rose also sent a smudged and dirty envelope, addressed to Margaret Morris, from which the stamp and postmark had been torn off. Once again, Rose told Maslow she had never shown the letter to Thomas Patrick or even told him about it.

By this time Hays was queasy about representing Thomas Patrick. If he proved he was the legitimate son of John G.—and he would have to be legitimate, since an illegitimate child could not inherit from his or her father—Morris was entitled to the $15 million estate John G. left on his death in 1914. In the absence of any will, his fortune had passed to his sisters and ultimately to Ella. And as a third-degree claimant, Morris would knock out more remote-degree, including the fifth-, sixth- and seventh-degree claimants Hays-Untermyer had so laboriously collected.

Hays decided to refer Morris to Raymond L. Wise, a young but able lawyer, formerly an assistant district attorney. To act as counsel, Wise engaged Joseph P. Martin, an Assistant District Attorney who practiced law part time, a practice permitted then. Hays gave Wise $750 from his disbursement fund to finance modestly the Morris claim for, as Hays states

April 6, 1897

Mrs Margaret Morris,

My Dear Friend.

I will be in Scotland for a visit sometime during the month of May or June. I only wish I could get matters straightened out here with my sisters, they are hard to reason with, I hope you have received my last remittance and that son, Thomas P. is behaving himself, I will close with best regards and fine health.

I remain

Your sincere friend,

John G. Wendel.

175 Bway.

N.Y. City.

The original letter dated April 6, 1897

in his book, "If they were able to gather substantial evidence, we would make some arrangement which would be to the advantage of all."

Neither Maslow nor Wise wrote Rose again to ask her to make any further search for documents. But in early 1932, Rose wrote to Maslow, announcing still another miracle:

> *Just a few lines to let you know I have searched every nook and corner as I was cleaning the house for the New Year, but I found no papers. But when I thought I looked everywhere, I remembered there was an old wooden box that my father kept his shoemaker's tools in. I emptied the contents out of the box and found this certificate underneath a sheet of brown paper, have sent it on to you hopeing [sic] you will receive it.*
>
> *I remain yours truly,*
> *Mrs. J. McAvan*

If Rose had been a literate woman, which she wasn't, one would have thought she was consciously emulating the Boswell Malahide papers found in an old croquet box some years before.

What she found was a marriage certificate, dated June 11, 1876, for John G. Wendel and Mary Ellen Devine, performed by the Pastor of Castle Garden, New York, James F. Calhoun, D.D., before two witnesses. Maslow turned over both the letter and the marriage certificate to Wise. And on May 7, 1932, Wise filed a duly verified Bill of Particulars on behalf of Thomas Patrick Morris, claiming in the third degree.

12.

SIFTING OUT UNSUCCESSFUL CLAIMANTS

It is a beautiful theory destroyed by an ugly fact.
OSCAR WILDE

With few exceptions, the hopeful heirs who alleged relationship to Ella proved their cases amply in the newspapers. Their cases did not fare nearly as well in the Surrogate's Court. For, when the moment of truth arrived—the filing of a verified Bill of Particulars—their claims turned out to be wishful thinking.

ELLA'S GRANDFATHER, JOHANN AND HIS ALLEGED MARRIAGES IN EUROPE

Mrs. Anna Bechler of Danzig, Germany, claimed to be a great-granddaughter of Johann. Her claim, in which she was represented by Colonel Lewis Landes, was based on his alleged marriage to a woman (whose name was unknown to Mrs.

Bechler) in Germany prior to his arrival in America in 1799. According to the claimant, Johann left behind a wife and two children, one who died in infancy and the other who was Mrs. Bechler's grandfather. This marriage would have made Johann's union with Elizabeth Astor bigamous—and the Wendel descendants illegitimate. But Mrs. Bechler never produced proof of the alleged marriage.

Mme. Francoise Amelie Wendel Rebling of Brussels, Belgium, also claimed to be a great-granddaughter of Johann by a marriage there, on August 16, 1792, to Mary Elizabeth Leydeck. The *New York Times* account stated that she was blind and penniless, unable to spend the necessary amounts to prove her claim. In her documents Johann had changed his name to Jean. But she had no proof of the marriage, and her story, even if accepted as true, made her a ninth-degree relative. In fact, Root Clark showed that she came from an entirely different family and was not related to Ella in any degree. Finally her attorneys withdrew her claim.

The most colorful story was the alleged marriage of Johann to Violet Wal Shinnecock, the Indian princess. This claim foundered on the ugly fact of complete lack of proof of the marriage in the Shinnecock tribal archives.

So Johann was not proved to be a bigamist when he married John Jacob Astor's half-sister, Elizabeth.

ELLA'S FATHER, JOHN D., AND HIS ALLEGED IRREGULAR SEXUAL PRACTICES

One John Saltsman Norris claimed descent from John D., who fathered an illegitimate child with Sarah Saltsman, his mother. He then sent her out to Ohio to live with her relatives, providing money for the child's support and visiting regularly.

There was no marriage certificate because there was no marriage. But Norris did have a declaration made by his mother:

> Sarah Saltsman was Born in Dubois Co Ind in 1818 my parents died when I was young. I went to New York to work out for a living while there I got with child by John D. Wendel and to keep down family trouble Wendel sent Sarah (me) Saltsman back to Duboise Co Indiana to my sister by the name of Enlow to stay till cnild was born. if it lived he was to come over to Indiana and setel with me for support of me and child, on November 14—1838 this child was born and in Dec 1838 John D. Wendel come to Indiana and seteled in the Duboise Co court for the child, with the understanding the child was to go by his mothers name so he was named John Saltsman. While the child was small 1839 Sarah (I) Saltsman married Thomas J. Norris and then I call him John Saltsman Norris and he always went by that name. This is the record of the birth of John Saltsman Norris written by his mother
>
> Sarah Norris
> in 1876.

He also produced a handwritten letter from John D. to his "illegitimate son":

> *New Yourk [sic]*
> *Oct 2 1848*
>
> *John Saltsman Norris*
>
> *My dear son*
>
> *I am sending you $12 dollars to get you some books and clothes for school. I am not very well have been sick for some time and am very nervous. I am planning to come to Ohio this winter on business if I do I will come and see you so be a good boy till I see you from your*
> *father*
> *John D. Wendel*

Unfortunately the ugly fact was John D's authentic handwriting did not remotely resemble the handwriting in the letter.

THE BREMEN WENDEL CLAIMANTS

Fifty-three persons in two groups, headed by Mrs. Gertrude Ohsann Kay of San Francisco and Adelaide Elizabeth Kroger of Bremen, laid claim to Ella's fortune. They were represented by Edward Bloom of San Francisco and Colonel Lewis Landes.

Their case never came before the Surrogate's Court. Because the records of the Wendel forebears, dating back to 1611, were found in St. Laurentius Evangelical Lutheran Church, they had a four-day hearing by the High District Court of Brandenburg, at Havelburg, Germany.

Judge Joachim Rudolphi of the High Court rendered a forty-six-page decision, replete with seals and stamps of the official German registry, with attached copies of the original church records. The ugly fact was since neither the Proponents nor anyone else in America had been made parties to the German proceeding, it was not at all binding on Surrogate Foley. And, more important, the closest relationship shown was the seventh-degree. According to the *New York Herald*, when these German claimants were told that Rosa Dew Stansbury, a fifth-degree claimant, had already proved her claim to Surrogate Foley's satisfaction,

> they said that a woman so old in the interior of America could hardly have such good papers to prove her ancestry as they had from Germany.

If Beckie had still been living, she would not have been happy to learn that, among their illustrious noble ancestors, according to the German proofs, one was Johann Gottfried Wendel, official executioner in Sandow, Germany, in 1800.

IRREGULAR SPELLINGS OF WENDEL

Some of the claimants were confident that Ella's grandfather, at some point, had altered the spelling of his name. One was Warren Olcott Wendell, of Sedalia, Missouri. The documentary evidence of his claim to the fortune consisted of an article in the *Kansas City Star* magazine of August 22, 1926:

> You do not find the Wendel sisters in the New York social register, but the name is ancient, and runs with distinction through the history of the state. The founder of the family came from Holland in 1640 when New York was New Amsterdam. He grew prosperous trading furs with the Indians, but others told him of the advantages of moving nearer to the wilderness and on their advice he went to Ft. Orange, what is now Albany. There Wendell—he spelled it with two "l's"—built a stout Dutch house under the guns of the fort, the idea being that since his kitchen chimney looked into the mouths of the cannon his house would not appeal to midnight scalping parties.
>
> This admirable arrangement was rudely upset by Governor Peter Stuyvesant, when he came stumping about the fort on his peg leg. Others had built homes under the guns. Stuyvesant ordered all the houses torn down and the sites cleared on the grounds that they might afford cover to attackers. Instead of a docile acquiescence Wendell and his fellow householders defended their cause with an independence that was little short of threatening. Their belligerence delighted the old warrior so that he paid the men handsomely for their houses and gave them generous grants of land farther from the fort.
>
> To this original heritage the Wendells added other fortunes by thrift and judicious marriages. A descendant moved to New England, where he became the sire of an illustrious line. The

strain crops up in the names of Oliver Wendell Holmes and Wendell Phillips. Unions were made with such lordly houses as the Schuylers, Van Dykes and Ten Broecks. Many Wendells migrated to Michigan, Minnesota and Kansas where they became staunch free-staters.

And New York wonders as the lives of these eccentric "old ladies" run out what strange things will be found in their wills.

The above is from the Kansas City Star Magazine of August 22, 1926, and is a small part of the whole article and other parts of the same article goes into considerable detail in showing the very odd characters of that Wendell family and how the daughters and sisters were what you might call brow beaten by their father and not allowed to marry but finally one of them married a man by the name of Swope and here I will mention that Mr. Swope's nephew is to get a nice rich plum in this will and is no blood kin at all. The brother of these sisters was one of the John Gottleb Wendells and he kept up the brow beating of his sisters and hampered them in every way and made recluses out of them and was very largely the cause of developing the sisters into very singular and cranks characters and what might be called hermits and recluses and this Kansas City Star article goes on to show many of the peculiarities that these sisters grew into from childhood on down the line to their final deaths and it should be sufficient proof when well proven that they were not of sound mind and could not make a real legal will. This last John Gottleb Wendell caused one of the sisters to be placed in a sanitarium some years ago when she came back from Europe and they claim she was insane as she had broken away from the despotism of her brother and gone to Europe without the consent of her brother and sister and she was very likely in a state of unsound mind before she went to Europe and after she came back and so they put her in a sanitarium and she died in 1926 or there abouts or sometime since that time and Mrs. Swope died last August.

There was 5 sisters and one brother and all records show that they were all queer and lived in deep gloom and seclusion with closed shutters in that old house at 5th Ave and 39th Street."

Secondly Warren submitted a statement that his mother had made before her death:

> There were two branches of the Wendell familys. Two brothers came from Holland, one settled in Connecticut, one in New York. The New York branch is the one that our family descended from, their Holland name was Vandell, in time changed to Wendell.
>
> Oliver Wendell Holmes and Wendell Phillips belong to the Connecticut branch. The New York ancestors are the ones that this family descended from. Your grandfather was Daniel Finch Wendell, born May 9, 1801. Born in East Orange, New York, came to Alton, Ill., in 1833, died December 16, 1869. The father of Daniel Finch Wendell was David Wendell, was born December 22, 1759. His father was John Wendell.

She went on to supply the Revolutionary and Civil War records of the Wendell family:

> My ancestors service in assisting in the establishment of American Independence during the war, the Revolution, were as follows:
>
> Daniel Finch was a lieutenant in Revolutionary War at the Massacre of Wyoming, was wounded in the thighs and later while kneeling in prayer in his cottage with his family was tomahawked by an Indian chief who broke into the room.
>
> The Finches were French Huguenotts.
>
> David Wendell belonged to Colonel Oliver Spencer's regiment, was wounded at battle of Germantown. Right arm was taken off above elbow. John Wendell enlisted under Baron Steuben. . . .
>
> Our own father was Wm. H. Wendell born in Upper Alton Ills and was in Civil War in 22nd Regiment of Ills volunteers, and he was promoted to rank of captain and served over four years in Army of Tennessee, and Cumberland under Gen Thomas Gen Rosecrans and Gen Grant and was on the staff of Gen Rosecrans,

> and in 7 big battles—and in the great battles at Lookout Mountain and Missionary Ridge and others.

But it could never be shown that Johann or his forebears ever spelled their name with two *l*s, or that any Wendels had come from Holland.

THE ALLEGED CHILDREN OF ELLA'S GREAT-AUNT, ELIZABETH WENDEL

Six people, represented by Irving H. Schaefer of New York and Representative Joe J. Manlove of Missouri, claimed to be grandchildren of Johann through Elizabeth Wendel, born in 1810. They alleged that Elizabeth, John D.'s sister and Ella's aunt, had been estranged from her family for many years and so was assumed dead. Not at all, they maintained. When Elizabeth was seventeen years old, her father, Johann, had objected to some acquaintance she had made, made their home unpleasant for her, and she had run away to Ohio. There she married Aaron Perry and bore six children, now staking their claim. In 1867, her brother, John D., learned of Elizabeth's new life and visited them in Ohio.

Their claim, as Abe Lincoln once said, was "as thin as the homeopathic soup that was made by boiling the shadow of a pigeon that had been starved to death." The ugly fact was that the Wendel family Bible showed Elizabeth had died in 1820, at the age of ten. Halstead, of Warren's office, had prepared an elaborate memorandum of other evidence, such as burial data, showing the Bible entry to be correct.

AN AUSTRALIAN CLAIMANT PRODUCED BY THE HAYS "TRIAL BALLOON"

After Hays, through a Forrest Davis story, invited Australian claimants to come forward, Untermyer received a letter from

Miss Mary Ellen Mann of Melbourne, Australia. She described herself as:

> the daughter of Nelson Blake Wendel and the niece of Elle and Lis. Brans Wendel, my mother, was the Grand Duke of Westminster's England daughter. I was born at my Grandfather's place the Hall of Westminster. My aunt told me when we met at Brighton Beach about 18 years ago, the time the will was made, that I had to receive everything after her death. That her brother, my father, married under another name but I am his daughter. I lived with my grandfather till I could walk about and one day my grandfather took me somewhere in a train to do some shopping and left me in a park and my uncle came along and picked me up and took me to New York. I lived there with my uncle and aunt Lis for a few years and my uncle brought me out here . . . did you find a note in her [my aunt's] stocking . . . my aunt Elle told me my father had me registered Maggie Wendel in England. . . .

Will Maslow's reply to the Untermyer office was:

1. Ella Wendel's only brother was named John Gottlieb and not Nelson Blake.

2. Ella spelled her name E-L-L-A and not E-L-L-E.

3. Even if John Gottlieb married under a different name, if he married the daughter of the Grand Duke of Westminster it would have been impossible to keep that marriage secret.

4. Although my knowledge of the nobility of England is of the slightest, I do not believe that there is a *Grand* Duke of Westminster although there is a Duke of Westminster, one of the wealthiest landowners of Great Britain.

5. I was also under the impression that the resort in England was called Brighton and not Brighton Beach.

6. Miss Mann's story that her Aunt Ella told her about the will eighteen years ago in which she promised to leave everything to her niece is fantastic, if not preposterous, and it is unlikely that Ella Wendel was ever at Brighton, England, or Brighton Beach, N.Y.

Maslow could have added that the Hall of Westminster, where Charles I was tried, was not equipped for birthing. Maslow's suggestion was that they ask Miss Mann for some documentary proof, which of course was never forthcoming.

THE "LINKOUS" DEW CLAIMANTS FROM WEST VIRGINIA

James Floyd Dew and William Robert Dew were both over eighty years of age when Ella died. Through their attorney, John E. Palmer, both laid claim to being fourth-degree relations to Ella.

Their claim rested on the allegation that their ancestor, John Hammond Dew, was a son of the marriage between James C. Dew and Harriet Stansbury Dew, and thus a half-brother of Mary Ann the Amiable. John Hammond Dew was born on September 17, 1813, in Baltimore. Instead of going to sea or to Australia, as the family tradition had it, these two aged Dew brothers said he went to Beckley, Virginia, because he had done something that "disgraced the family." Whether he left home voluntarily or was ejected, the claimants were not certain. Out of shame, he changed his name to Benjamin R. Linkous. In 1846 or 1847, he entered into a common-law marriage with a distant cousin, Mary Dew, and fathered the two Dew claimants around 1850. Still, if their claim was valid, given their advanced age, both claimants were one degree closer to Ella than Rosa Dew Stansbury and the Barney claimants.

Linkous was a schoolteacher and a surveyor; he fought with the U.S. Army in the 1847 war against Mexico. After the Civil War, in which he served the Confederacy as a colonel, Linkous left his common-law wife and married Susan Johnson, by whom he had a son, Charles Linkous. After Susan's death, he married a woman named Augusta, and died when he was past seventy.

According to the claimants, Benjamin Linkous had eventually reconciled with his family. General Stansbury had visited Beckley and given his grandson money. James Floyd Dew, who was then twelve years old, vividly remembered when "Uncle Car" (Carville Stansbury) visited in 1861, since Uncle Car had given him money as well. But documents that might have proved the relationship did not exist—they were destroyed, the brothers said, when the Beckley home (then in West Virginia) was torched by Northern troops during the Civil War. They could substantiate their claim only with the rather vague testimony of their ancient peers, who had known Linkous in his old age.

It would be difficult to disprove their claim, but Harlan was not deterred. He dispatched Robbins and Strube to West Virginia to do the genealogical digging, and Laporte of the Root Clark Washington office to get certified copies of the census records. Laporte also unearthed a veterans administration application by Margaret A. Linkous, widow of Benjamin R. Linkous, for an increase of his Mexican War service pension—but the name Margaret was unknown to the claimants. Clearly they had not done their homework carefully enough in fabricating the Linkous history.

Meanwhile, Robbins and Strube had taken statements from people in Christianburg, Virginia, and Beckley, West Virginia, that Benjamin was a real Linkous and not John Hammond Dew. Various other records placed his birth in Virginia, not in Baltimore. But the clincher came from the photographs Robbins had taken of the family burial plot on the old Linkous farm at Matamoras, Montgomery County, Virginia. There the grave of Thomas Linkous was inscribed *Father of Benjamin R*, and Benjamin's own tombstone stated his date of birth as April 25, 1825. When confronted with this, the claimants maintained that Benjamin had adopted a birthdate eleven years later to conceal his real identity as a Dew—hardly a convincing argument. But why would he have changed the month and day of birth from September 17 to April 25? The house of cards was beginning to tumble down.

By now Harlan was convinced that he could show Palmer, the Dews's attorney, that their claim was totally devoid of merit. When Robbins met with Palmer and laid all his cards on the table, Palmer surrendered. He withdrew the claim grudgingly; in his statement to the court he affirmed his belief in his clients but was unable to prove their fourth-degree relationship.

THE "GOOD SAMARITAN LETTER" CLAIMANTS TO ELLA'S FORTUNE

Nineteen Wendel claimants from the Midwest, who were represented by Boker & Epstein, alleged they were seventh-degree relations of Ella. They traced their relationship through an inscription on a leaf of an old German Bible, allegedly written by Jahn (not "Johann") Gottleib Mathias Wendel, Ella's grandfather. He had purportedly given the Bible to his nephew, Michael Daniel Wendel, the grandfather of the nineteen claimants.

In August 1932, Surrogate Foley disallowed the claims of all those more remote than the fifth-degree, including these nineteen clients of Boker & Epstein. And then a miracle occurred. One of the nineteen discovered in a trunk new evidence showing that all of them were related in the fifth-degree to Ella. So their attorney, Jacob H. Epstein, filed an affidavit to have Foley modify his prior order and permit the nineteen persons to file new Bills of Particulars.

The new evidence consisted of three letters and a will, all written in German, translated by two professors of German at the University of Illinois. The first, "The Good Samaritan Letter," from Ella's grandfather, "Jahn," to his "nephew

Markus," gave him $900,000 or "9.000.000,"—the letter stating both figures —for saving his life.

July 20, 1837
New York
Fifth Avenue and 39th St.

Dear Nephew Markus Daniel Wendel:

At last I am going to answer your long letter which I have received a few days ago. My health is better since I am away from Chilcati, Ohio. I shall forget [Translator's note: Apparently the word "never" is left out here] when I had those cramps and cold chills after I had eaten the fish and had drunk milk, beer and wine together. I thought I would stay dead, I was so sick and blown up, when I had taken a little of the old man's beverage. He had poured wine, beer and whiskey together, which made me so sick when I drank it. I had cramps and I was swollen up by it and could get no breath, I lay down in the grass on my stomach and was terribly sick. You came to me and ask me whether I was sick, I said I have such pains, you said I was really sick and you told the young people to go home. Then they all did go home and I thought that I could not make the mile to your house. Then I took soda-ginger, but I could not take much because I was so cold. When I was at your house you gave me soda and ginger and I had to put my feet in hot water. You heated turpentine oil and camphor and you rubbed me with it. I became more swollen up all the time and Mr. Wetzel fetched two doctors and they said I had blood poisoning from eating fish and drinking milk and beer after as this makes poison and the doctor said that I would stay dead. It was 10 o'clock when you again started to rub me. The doctors had left. You said you would restore me to health, the whole night you worked on me not losing one minute. This has done me good. You have rubbed me with this oil and have given me hot tea which made me feel somewhat better, but the cramps were the same. I felt so bad that I had no hope. You came again and massaged me. I told you that I would rather stay dead, then you said that you would make me feel better. You said I would get better and I said no. For some minutes the pains were gone but then they came back. You have taken much trouble with me and I shall never forget it. You gave me hot tea which made me warm. If you had not done all that for me I believe I would have died, I could get no breath. I am deeply indebted to you for you have saved my life. The whole day you were working to make me better and I shall pay you well for that. I have often said to my son: John Daniel I would have died if my nephew Markus Daniel Wendel had not helped me and saved my life and he has done so much to get me back to health that I shall never forget it and never again shall I eat fish and drink milk and beer together. This made the poison in the stomach and that is bad. I have suffered terribly for eight hours, it was a matter of life and death and I owe my life to you as I have already said. The last that you did for me—I still see you running in the dark night and you cut off elderberries. When you came into the house again I asked you where you had been and I was surprised. You put a tube on the elderberries and put that into me in order to get the gas out and the gas escaped very quickly and I got better. The next day I had much rumbling in the bowels and [one word illegible] because you had left the tube in me so long. That was better than all the pain and I was no longer swollen up and I keep the tube when I swell up again. And now Markus Daniel Wendel I give you 9.000.000 Dollars of my cash money because you have helped me so well. It was a matter of life and death and I said to my son John Daniel Wendel that I owe this to you and that you should have it because you have saved my life and this is my will after my death or after my son has died when the last grandchildren are dead. I want you and your children and your grandchildren to inherit everything, both money and land as I have provided in my will. I do not want my money and property to go to the institutions or to some other country. I owe them nothing and I wish that everything goes to my blood relatives Markus Daniel Wendel's children and grandchildren and not to Germany. I have run away from Germany and so have my brother Johann Jacopsen Wendel who is your father, and my brother Juergen Henry Wilhelm, we all have run away from Germany. There are seven years which is the law in Germany, they consider you dead. . . . I have often said at the house of my nephew Markus Daniel Wendel that I would rather be dead. You have never asked me for anything, you have helped me much, your wife Maria also, and I shall not forget it as long as I live. . . . You have helped me much, you said that I would stay dead when you gave me the tube, then I got better and the pains disappeared. At 5 o'clock I was better and I wanted to play you something on the violin [some words illegible] I had to laugh but I did not feel like it, and my family said. You will get the 9.000.000 Dollars, nine hundred thousand dollars and I want to put my affairs in order in a year and not later than two years and I want you to take a good lawyer who does not demand too much and stay out of court. Markus Daniel Wendel, you are the only blood relative I have in America and I want you and your children and your grandchildren to inherit everything; when my son Jan Daniel Wendel and all my grandchildren are dead then every thing I leave I want my nephew Markus Daniel Wendel, his children and grandchildren to get. It is all for you. I have enclosed my will in this letter and have written down this will in this letter. I want you to keep this letter with my will carefully, and no other will is valid. Only the will which I have made is of value. I have told you already that my estate shall not go to some other country for instance Germany or to the institutions, I do not owe them anything. I have earned all of this money in America and I wish that it stays in this country, and the blood relatives, the Wendels, shall have it, you in the first place. . . . Whoever has my will in his hand and this letter also I wish that he make this letter public so that he will get his right to all my money and buildings. You are the only blood relatives I have in America. It is my wish that my blood relatives Markus Daniel Wendel and his children and grandchildren get my estate as stated above, and nobody else. There are nine children in our family, I have written them all down in the old Bible which I have given you; I am writing them down again, these are all my brothers and sisters and they are all your aunts and uncles.

From your Uncle Jahn Gottlieb Mattias Wendel born 1767 to my nephew Markus Daniel Wendel born 1803.

Cornelius Christian Wendel born 1775
Jurgen Henry Wilhelm Wendel born 1779
Jahn Daniel Wendel born 1779
Anna Dorothea Wendel born 1777
Jahn Gottlieb Mattias Wendel born 1767
Johann Jacopsen Wendel born 1773
Johann Christian Wendel born 1770
Johann Andreas Wendel born 1772
Chatharina Wendel born 1773

Markus Daniel Wendel come soon to New York. I shall come next summer, hoping to see you again.
I am your Uncle Jahn Gottlieb
Mattias Wendel

39 Street Fifth Avenue"

To this letter Johann had appended his "will":

To my nephew Markus Daniel Wendel

My nephew Markus Daniel Wendel, his children, his grandchildren shall inherit my estate and everything that belongs to it. It is my wish that the last ones who are alive or whoever it is who has possession of this will go forward with it, and keep the will, and get a good lawyer who does not demand too much money and have it settled in one year or not later than two years. This is my last will. This is my last word. All other wills are invalid. I subscribe this for my son John Daniel Wendel Jahn Gottlieb Mattias Wendel. My grandchildren they shall all get their share and no other will but this one which I have written myself [a few words unintelligible].

Jahn Gottlieb Mattias Wendel.

Not content with this fine letter, a translation of a letter written in German from John G., Ella's brother, to his cousin was also produced by the claimants:

June 11, 1891

Dear Cousin Franklin Wendel:

We are all slow now since you have gone back to work in Chicago, I would have been glad to go with you for a visit and I shall do this the next time when you come back to New York. Do not let me wait so long, we had so much fun when you were here. I had to laugh as never in my life. You told me how you boys all went fox hunting in the field during the night. You laughed permanently; I would like to be with you when you go fox hunting again, I have never seen anything like that before. I cannot understand why you go hunting during the night and the boys have to climb into the trees and shake down the coons and the one pole cat. I would not go up into the tree to shake them down and you said how they fell out of the tree, how the dogs caught them but they let them go again and you said it had smelled so that you all had the odor on you for weeks. I had to laugh so much when you called the horses all old [one word illegible] and you would not pay $10 a piece for them. I know that the horses are better in the country as they get grass and good pasture there; I think where the horse [rest of the sentence unintelligible]. I have seen it myself and you said about the old cabs that you would rather walk than take a ride in them. I had to laugh when you said that the seat of them was so high that it was dangerous to fall down between the horses and you said that the old fat horses made so much noise with their feet as if they were going to run away. You said that you could drive no horse in the country, not so fast that it would run away. You said that you had a beautiful black horse which could make a mile in three minutes and it is a good horse and very fat. I shall come out into the country soon when you return home. You said that you have no mountains in Illinois, the roads are good but not paved. You said that the cement pavement spoils the feet of the horses and that they would rather go on *a sandy road. Cousin Franklin I had to laugh when you were in Chilicothe [sic], Ohio, I ate such big meals, chickens, dumplings and noodles as never in my life. Every where we were we had much to eat and dancing during the night and the dust was so thick in the house from the dancing one could hardly see with whom one danced. I wish I were present again, I like chickens and dumplings and noodles. They said you must stay longer than two weeks and no go away before that. [some words illegible]. No wonder you made so much fun for us. Nobody here liked it when you left us. You want to know whether we have eaten all the head cheese in the big pig's stomach when you were gone. You said that that was the biggest head cheese you had ever seen. We have always made it at home and had it in the smoke for the winter. Cousin Franklin we spoke of all our relatives and you said that you have not seen all your relatives. We have so many cousins and double cousins and you are wondering that I [words missing in the original]. Your grandfather Markus Daniel Wendel is my uncle and your grandfather; and we soon talked about the old will; my grandfather Jahn Gottlieb Mathias Wendel talked about the will he had made and he wants your grandfather Markus Daniel Wendel [some words unintelligible]. The will said that all real and personal property should be divided between my son Johan Daniel Wendel and my grandchildren and my nephew Markus Daniel Wendel, his children and grandchildren according to justice.*

Your grandfather [Translator's note: The context requires here my grandfather*] Gottlieb Jahn Mathias Wendel bequeathed to your grandfather nine hundred thousand 9.000.000 Dollars because he has saved his life when he was lying between life and death for eight hours and he wanted your grandfather to have this money who is my uncle. . . . Johann Gottlieb Mathias Wendel has made this will in 1837 and he wants it to stand and nobody shall make any other will, his son Jahn Daniel Wendel or his grandchildren or whoever it may be. He wants the will to remain in force which he has made in 1837. Jahn Gottlieb Mathias Wendel wants to have all other wills broken as my father Jahn Daniel Wendel has told us so often. He said that he* *would make no other will and he does not want his children to make any other will. The one which his father Jahn Gottlieb Mathias Wendel should stand. It should not go to public institutions or other countries. He said that he owed them nothing, that he earned this money in America and that it stays here. . . . People always said Jahn why do you not make a will, I said I need no will, this is not the business of other people, my grandfather Jahn Gottlieb Mathias Wendel has made his will. we know it all and no other will is necessary. His will shall remain in force and none other and all other wills which may be made by other people are worth nothing. My grandfather always said that he who gets in touch with this will shall take a lawyer and not go into court, I want my estate settled within one year and not later than two years, My grandfather Markus Daniel Wendel [Translator's note: The context requires* your*] has always mentioned this old will to my father in the long letters which he always wrote that he wanted it that way. When my father Jahn Daniel Wendel said his father Jahn Gottlieb Mathias Wendel can do as he pleases, my father wanted your grandfather Markus Daniel Wendel to have nine hundred thousand dollars, his nephew and his children and grandchildren shall have it, everything after his death, his estate shall go to them. . . . My sisters can make no other will after my death and my father Jahn Daniel Wendel has always said make no other will, and cousin Franklin if you are still alive come forward with this old will, or his sister or brothers should take a good lawyer and show this will to anybody in the family. You must insist on your rights and you shall have it because my grandfather said that this is his will and it shall be distributed accordingly and do everything you can when the time comes. [Some words unintelligible] And Cousin Franklin, this is how I want it [some words unintelligible] as a will is a will and it makes no difference how old it is and who gets it into his hands he should go with it to the court [some words unintelligible]. You grandchildren have a right to it and be careful that the lawyer will not cheat you out of it. You must insist on your rights . . . Cousin Franklin you would like to know whether I have gone to Germany again. I* *have been there twice but do not like it. I was in no other country before. I do not like the long ocean voyage. Now Franklin you do as I have written in this letter when the time comes. This is the truth regarding the will that it should go to no institutions or other countries, we owe them nothing. It goes to our blood relatives, the Wendels. Cousin Franklin you are more like a brother to me than a cousin, I wish that you would live nearer so that we can see each other more frequently. I had always so much fun when you were here. You made us all laugh. You said after I have gone to the country I would not like it anymore in New York. You say that you go fishing and swimming in the river. Cousin Franklin you said why didn't you take a wife. He always said he wanted no wife. I am now fifty years old and I am like you. I want no wife and even if she were hung with gold. I am like you I want to remain the master and need no other master. I see no woman who laughs and says marrying is a vice forever and I shall rather remain an old bachelor and go where ever I please.*

Hope to see you again. Answer soon.

From your cousin Jahn Gottlieb Wendel
New York, 5 Ave, 39 St.

To my Cousin Franklin Wendel.

And finally Ella, whom one would think would not write her name "Elle," wrote in German to her cousin and a translation was produced by the claimants.

July 10, 1891

To Franklin Wendel.

My dear cousin I want to write you a few lines in order to tell you that I have forgotten the books which John gave you to take them to Chicago. You said that you would not forget them. The old fiction stories I shall send by mail today, you need not return them as we have read them all. Your brother Johann said that you should soon come again. We had so much pleasure and enjoyment when you were here and do not wait so long with your visit. Johann had to laugh about the pictures of the old spinsters. They were as ugly as I have ever seen any in my life. If you go out with them people will think that you come from a theatre party. You said that the girls in Chicago were wearing long dresses and that it takes you some time to get them out of the way when you dance with them otherwise you would fall down. You said that you would not want a girl from the city, they dance all night and sleep during the day and cannot cook nor keep house. You said there are no pretty girls in Chicago and New York and that it is better not to get married. Cousin Franklin we spoke of our relatives and you said that you do not know them all. You have so many married cousins and uncles and grandmothers. You said you would not want to marry a relative even if she were hung with gold and you ask how I am related to your grandfather Markus Daniel Wendel and you said uncle Markus and my father Jahn Daniel Wendel were first cousins to your grandfather Markus Daniel Wendel. The two have married sisters. My mother's name was Marian Due . . . My aunt Maria Due Desto had gone to Germany for a visit and [Translator's note: Presumably the word met *is left out here) your grandfather Markus Daniel Wendel and she married him in Germany who is my uncle Markus. My Uncle Markus always said that my Aunt Maria was a pretty woman. It was love at first sight. They were married on January 14, 1830 and in later years they came to America to live. Cousin Franklin, your father Johann Jacopsen Wendel knows that our mothers were sisters. Cousin Johann Jacopsen, your father said I look much more like his mother than my own mother. Cousin Franklin, there are six children in your father's family, Johann Jacopsen, who is your father and his brothers and sisters. I am the last and the youngest of them and we are all first cousins to you. We are all first cousins to your father Johann Jacopsen Wendel born 1883. We are cousins a second time by our mothers being sisters.*

Cousin Franklin you know my grandfather Johann Gottlieb Mathias Wendel made a will and we all know it, in 1838. Our father Jahn Daniel Wendel said so often what was in this will and my father always said he did not want to make any other will only what his father had made, Jahn Gottlieb Mathias Wendel and he wants to have it distributed as he has made it. Our house on Fifth Avenue and 39th Street shall also be justly distributed and my grandfather who was Johann Gottlieb Mathias Wendel does not want any of his property to go to the institutions in this or any other country. He does not owe them anything. He often said it should go to his blood relatives Johann Daniel Wendel, his grand children, his nephew Markus Daniel Wendel and his children and grandchildren, and he wills to your grandfather Markus Daniel Wendel nine hundred thousand dollars 9.000.000 dollars as a reward for having saved his life when two doctors had given him up with fish poisoning . . . and my father Johann Daniel Wendel said he would make no other will and he does not want his children to make any other will, but if they do it anyway it is his wish that it shall not be valid and no other will shall be made but the one made by his father Jahn Gottlieb Mathias Wendel, and he always said that it makes no difference how old the will is that a will is a will and he wants this to stand and no other will should be made in later years by my son Johann Daniel Wendel or my grandchildren. . . . My father always said that his father's will should stand and be carried out as he has made it in 1837. . . . The people say why do you girls make no wills, we said that we need no wills. I told nobody that my grandfather Jahn Gottlieb Mathias Wendel has already made a will just as he wants to have it distributed and we children want it to remain so. My brother Johann has always said that his grandfather's Johann Gottlieb Mathias Wendel will should stand and my father Johan Daniel Wendel has made no other will, my grandfather's will shall be carried out, as he has earned the money and can do with it as he pleases. . . . My father Johan Daniel Wendel has always said that his father Johann Gottlieb Mathias Wendel wants his will carried out that his estate should go to his blood relatives, the Wendels in America and he said that his nephew Markus Daniel Wendel is the only blood relative we had in America to visit and he has visited his nephew

Markus Daniel Wendel every summer and they had a good time in the country in the summer, and your grandfather Markus Daniel Wendel who is my uncle came to the City of New York in the winter and he said that he could not get away in the summer because he had so much work to do during that time. Cousin Franklin come soon again.

From your cousin Elle von (?) Wendel
New York, Fifth Avenue 39th St

To My Cousin Franklin Wendel.

The evidence brought forward by Root Clark on the hearing before Foley made mincemeat of these fictitious letters. While Johann wrote German and John G. could but seldom did, Ella couldn't; and the appearance of the same mistake in the three letters (*nine hundred thousand* and *9.000.000*) make the inference irresistible that all three were written by the same hand—a forger's. And how on earth could Johann in 1837 have been aware that all his money went to "public institutions or other countries" in 1931 under Ella's will? He would have to have been a Nostradamus. Or John G. be aware of that fact in 1891? And why did John G. and Ella call their mother "Mary Ann Due"? And why do the letters say John D., Ella's father, made no will when he clearly did?

Elbridge Stein, an expert on questioned documents, appears in the Wendel Estate for the first time to testify all three letters were written by the same hand.

The New York Times quoted Harlan as "expressing astonishment that such letters were offered in evidence by members of the bar. He declared that if it was not fraudulent then it was the work of some person suffering from a mental disorder."

After two days of hearings, Boker and Epstein realized that they had been duped and withdrew the claim and also withdrew as attorneys for the 19 claimants. For the really ugly fact was the address of Johann's 1837 letter.

Surrogate Foley wrote:

> The newly discovered letters . . . are not only suspicious in appearance but are palpable fabrications. Typical of their character is one letter written by John G.M. Wendel . . . dated July 20, 1837, and contains the address of the writer as "New York, 39 Street, Fifth Ave"! The documentary proof in the record before me, particularly the deeds, show the absurdity of this statement. The Wendel property at 39 Street and 5th Avenue was not acquired until between 1845 and 1847, at least 9 years after the date of the letter. It was acquired not by the alleged writer of the letter, but by his son, John D. Wendel. The family home was not built until about 1850, at least 14 years after the date which appears on the letter.

Foley impounded the letters with the thought that a criminal prosecution might be brought, but none ever was. So ended the career of a promising writer of fictional letters.

CLAIMANT CALLING ELLA'S GRANDFATHER AN IMPOSTOR

Ernst Friedrich Carl Wendel had a most ingenious theory—that Ella's grandfather was an impostor. A former waiter and cheese salesman, Wendel had served as a steward on the American liner *St. Louis* in 1895. He had been fortuitously transferred there from another ship, one hour before its departure from Europe. Rebecca, Ella's sister, was a passenger. Ernst claimed that he had met Rebecca on board and that she had assured him of her belief that he belonged to her family.

Ernst's grandfather, John Gottlieb Mathias Wendel, the son of Arend Wendel, had been born in Stralsund, Germany. The Proponents repeatedly told Ernst that Ella's father used his middle name, *Gottlob*, interchangeably with *Gottleib*. Ernst violently disagreed, insisting that they were two different people. To clinch his argument, he quoted Rebecca, now conveniently dead, as having said:

> My grandfather was John Gottlieb Matthias Wendel and your great-grandfather, John Wendel, were children of Arend and Maria Meier Wendel and therefore they are yours and our great-grandparents in common. Your great-grandfather was born in Stralsund. For my grandfather's papers, thousands of dollars have been spent but all in vain.
>
> Now remember if you ever have to use this, there is a party in Altona who has for years annoyed the family. Understand this party is an impostor. Therefore will you swear to me as a Wendel, for the Wendel I know you are, that you will never allow any one to defame our and your grandparents' honorable name.

Unfortunately, the ugly fact was that he never produced any proof beyond this remembered snatch of conversation.

CAROLINE WELLBORN DEW, A LATE-FILING CLAIMANT

Among the horde of Dew claimants who filed claims in the estate was Caroline Wellborn Dew. According to an interview in the *World-Telegram* of October 1932, she sat quietly and patiently on the sidelines while over two thousand claimants pushed, jostled, and shoved to get their hands on Ella money. Finally the propitious moment arrived. Her close friend, Evangeline Adams, the noted astrologer, told her to put her claim in the hands of George Gordon Battle, an eminent attorney. At first Battle wished to shield his aristocratic client from the fierce publicity of the early stages of the contest. But at the appropriate time he duly filed her claim in the Surrogate's Court.

She was an author and an active worker against the Prohibition amendment; her principal pastime was dog breeding. Dubbing her "Blue Book Leader" in the headline, the *World-Telegram* reported she had traced her lineage:

> through an amazing group of ancestors, including officers in Washington's army, whose papers were signed by Lighthorse Harry Lee, a Governor of Georgia, two U.S. Senators and even to John Marshall, Chief Justice of the United States Supreme Court.
>
> Seated in her studio at the antique, claw-legged mahogany table upon which William Dew signed the papers which deferred the Civil War for a decade, Miss Dew admitted that she would press her claim to the limit.
>
> "What will I do if I am awarded the Wendel wealth," she repeated a question that was put to her. "Well, it's a large question, but I'm sure it will be well spent.
>
> "I believe I'll run my pet bulldog for president," she said, playfully stroking the animal at ther feet. "You see he's an ardent wet, and I am utterly opposed to prohibition."

But however wellborn she was, she could not prove she was well connected to Ella.

THE FORGED TOMBSTONE CLAIMANTS

A tombstone in the private burial plot of the Stansbury family in Baltimore showed that James C. Dew and his wife Henrietta had a son, Thomas, brother of Mary Ann the Amiable. He was born October 6, 1808, and died on August 7, 1812, when he was nearly four. But two Dew brothers claimed that, in fact, Thomas had survived. He had gone to Mississippi, where he had fathered a family and died in 1857. The two claimed to be his bona-fide grandsons and Ella's heirs in the fifth degree.

From the beginning, Schwabe suspected the claim, first because there might be any number of Thomas Dews—none necessarily the resurrected four-year-old child. Secondly, the Mississippi tombstone was new, allegedly replacing the original, which had fallen into ruinous condition. Then too, although the brothers' original claim cited July 30, 1806, as Thomas's birthday, the genealogical chart Root Clark later supplied to the Surrogates Court placed his parents' marriage on September 27, 1807—a fact theretofore apparently unknown to these claimants.

While it would be hard enough to get a court to accept that Thomas did not die at age four, it would be impossible also to get the court to swallow the assertion that he was born out of wedlock too. Hence the new tombstone amended the date to August 30, 1808, postponing his birth by twenty-five months to make him legitimate.

Given these facts, the Dew brothers' claim received short shrift from the Proponents.

13.

SURROGATE FOLEY MOVES DECISIVELY

The world has got to move. As the Supreme Court has said in some of its decisions, estates have to be settled.
SURROGATE FOLEY

Even without these spurious claims, there were still more than two thousand others to be processed, beginning with those alleging close relations to Ella. So, in June 1932, Foley began by identifying the nearest alleged relatives whose claims would be tried before him. These were:

Third Degree:	Thomas Patrick Morris
Fourth Degree:	Three other persons, who withdrew their claims for failure of proof
Fifth Degree:	Rosa Dew Stansbury, the eight Barney claimants, the six Dew sisters from Tennessee, and ten others who also withdrew their claims

For Rosa's claim, there was no contest, since Root Clark had already conceded her relationship. The time had arrived to establish the eight Barneys' claim of fifth-degree relationship to Ella. Under Harlan's direction, Robbins and Schwabe had researched their history thoroughly. Root Clark presented to Foley an eight-page memorandum tracing the infant, George Stiles Dew, through his metamorphosis into John Holland Barney, Jr., and then through the rest of his life—his two marriages, the birth of his children, and his eventual death. Bolstered with guardianship accounts, deeds, census data, etc., the memorandum continued to track the family through two succeeding generations, up to the claimants themselves.

This research basically supported the Barney claim—with one hitch. The children of Benjamin Morgan Barney and Sarah J. Moore Barney, who had settled with the Proponents for $25,000 each, were the offspring of Benjamin's second marriage. There was oral evidence that he had divorced his first wife, but no documentary proof. The documents had probably been destroyed in the San Francisco earthquake and fire of 1906.

Representing Barney clients who descended from the first marriage, Hays and Untermyer argued that, without documentary proof of Benjamin Morgan Barney's divorce, descendants from the second marriage could not prove their fifth-degree relationship. Foley rejected that argument. Both parties to the divorce had acknowledged it, for both remarried, Benjamin Morgan Barney in a religious ceremony in the presence of several members of his family. The validity of the second marriage had stood unchallenged for more than fifty years. To deny its validity now would brand these children illegitimate, which Foley refused to do.

So, by upholding their claim, Foley established that there were nine people with fifth-degree relationship to Ella.

Then he decided to dismiss the more than two thousand claims alleging relationship in the sixth or more-remote degree. He had Root Clark print an order requiring those obscure Wendels, Dews, Stansburys and others to show cause why their claims should not be dismissed. The printed schedule, listing the names of the claimant and the names and addresses of their attorneys, was fifty-six pages long.

So on the fateful day of August 11, 1932, the courtroom was packed with lawyers, and in many cases their clients, to hear the death knell of their fantasies of becoming rich. Judge Friendly recalls telling the Root Clark office that he would be back within the hour, and when the calendar was called, he moved that the claims be dismissed. "No, Mr. Friendly," said Foley, "that is not the way we are going to do it. We are going to have the clerk read each claimant's name, and the name and address of his or her lawyer." Judge Friendly remembers listening to the drone of names for almost a full day. Of course, some of the attorneys took exception and threatened to appeal the dismissal—but none ever did.

And so, more than two thousand claimants—asserting relationship to Ella ranging from the sixth to the thirteenth degree—vanished from the scene. In one stroke, the vast field was reduced to sixteen. They were the nine fifth-degree relations whose claims had already been established, the six Tennessee Dew claimants, and, most important of all, Thomas Patrick Morris.

14.

THE SIX TENNESSEE DEW SISTERS

"I have spoken of this delusion or obsession of these ladies that they were related to Ella Wendel. I find now that to it has been added—I do not say directly through them—an imposition upon the Court by fabricated evidence."
SURROGATE FOLEY AT A HEARING
MARCH 30, 1933

Six Dew sisters from Tennessee had filed claims of fifth-degree relationship to Ella, through their grandfather, one "John H. Dew." If his middle name had been "Hammond" he would have been John Hammond Dew, Ella's uncle. Unfortunately, his middle name had been "Howel" (sometimes spelled "Howell"), but it took three separate court hearings, a genealogist fabricating documents, discovery of the old original tombstone on his grave, and an angry Surrogate Foley referring the matter to the Grievance Committee of the Bar Association before the Dew sisters ceased from their efforts to confuse the situation by making two separate persons into one.

The John Hammond Dew ("John Hammond") who was the brother of Mary Ann the Amiable, Ella's mother, set sail for Australia as a young man and was never heard from again. There are conflicting geneological Wendel notes as to the manner of his perishing, Rebecca stating he died of yellow fever in Australia, and Ella telling Warren that he was lost at sea before he arrived there.

The six Dew sisters, who were represented by George Gordon Battle, had as their grandfather, John Howel Dew, who was born on January 18, 1802—perhaps 1803—married Rebecca Houston at Columbia, Tennessee, on June 14, 1836, and died there on March 5, 1844. But the Wendel and Rebecca Swope Bibles show their Dew uncle was born on September 17, 1813—11½ years after John Howel.

Once again Root Clark faced the chore of tracing events that happened more than a century before. And once again Robbins and Schwabe, under the direction of Harlan and MacLean, proved equal to the task. By the time the claim was scheduled for hearing on October 10, 1932, Battle had withdrawn as counsel, presumably because he doubted that he could prove his case. With a new lawyer, George A. Washington, with Horace A. Gray as his counsel, the hearing proceeded before Foley on December 21, 1932.

The claimants' only proof that their grandfather was really named John Hammond was the oral testimony of two of the sisters, based on declarations by certain other relatives.

The Proponents had meticulously researched the life history of John Howel Dew. In the War Department records, they found a pension application made by his mother, Nancy Tower Wright Dew, in May 17, 1851, based on the Revolutionary War service of her husband, Reverend John Dew, originally of Georgia and then of Wilson County, Tennessee. Attached to the application was a page from her family Bible, showing the birth of John H. Dew, "son of Jno Dew and Nancy, his wife . . . the 18th day of Jany 1802." And when Reverend John Dew died in 1823, he left a will, unearthed by Robbins, making a bequest to his son John *Howel* Dew. It was beginning to seem obvious that John Howel Dew and John Hammond Dew were two separate people.

The evidence kept mounting. Court records showed that John H. Dew and his brother Mathew posted a bond as executors of their father's will in Wilson County in 1823—at this time, John Hammond was only ten years old. And he posted another bond four years later—John Hammond was only fourteen—to serve as guardian of two infant children, along with his brother-in-law, William L. Sypert. Then in 1831, he served in the House of Representatives of Tennessee, when John Hammond was only eighteen.

But then John Howel moved in 1837 from Wilson County to Maury County, Tennessee, and Robbins and Schwabe followed his trail. He was admitted to the bar there the same year; census records for 1840 show his name and his age between thirty and forty years (John Hammond would have been only twenty-seven years old); the *Journal of the Tennessee House of Representatives* (1841–1842) show him as a member from Maury County; and many court documents arising from his activities as a member of the Maury County Bar showed that the claimants' grandfather was an entirely separate and distinct person from John Hammond, who had disappeared and was presumed dead.

Then a problem that had previously plagued the Proponents arose again—a new tombstone. It had been erected after Ella died, surely a most suspicious action. Warren wrote to Washington:

> I am told that Miss Hattie Dew said that there are three John H. Dew gravestones; that the first one is in her possession at her home and that Mr. Robbins was not permitted to examine

> it; that the W. M. Dean Marble Company of Columbia, Maury County, took up this stone for the Dews on November 3, 1931, a date subsequent to the death of Miss Ella Wendel. I think that my representative should be permitted to see the stone now in the possession of Miss Hattie Dew; also any third stone not standing in the Dew Cemetery plot in Columbia, Tennessee. If you have photographs of these tombstones, I think that I should be furnished with copies of all of them.

This was followed by a conference between Washington and Friendly at which all of the evidence unearthed by Robbins and Schwabe was put on the table. Washington produced a photograph of the original tombstone. There were only two tombstones, not three. The original showed that Colonel John H. Dew "departed this life on the 5 of March 1844, aged 43 years . . ." So, according to the inscription, he had been born in 1801—twelve years before John Hammond's birth and six years before John Hammond's parents were married.

As Washington explained and his clients testified at the hearing, the colonel's wife was older than he and so had antedated his tombstone to reduce the disparity in age. But Foley was hardly convinced. Aside from the other findings, Root Clark had also gathered personal documents spanning John H. Dew's life, including his will. Every one bore the signature as *John H. Dew*—never *John Hammond Dew*. Foley therefore held that the claimants were not related to Ella, and disallowed their claims.

Amazingly, the sisters persevered—and a "miracle" occurred. They had hired Robert E. Landis, a genealogist of Nashville, Tennessee, and Detroit, Michigan, who had proved a veritable Merlin. New evidence he discovered provided grounds, they said, for a new hearing. The new documents, claimed Washington's affidavit, came from the files of the Chancery Court in Maury County and were signed *Jno Hammond Dew*.

Landis, who had come to genealogy from the garage and real estate business, proceeded to Maury County, Tennessee, where he found in the Chancery Court files a "copy" of a decree signed *Jno Hammond Dew*. Landis received permission, granted as a matter of course as the then-current clerk of the court testified, to have a photostat made of the document and seven others from the files. The photostats were certified by the clerk on February 8, 1933, and the originals locked in a file cabinet. But the next morning, when the clerk fetched the originals to show them to his local judge, one signed decree was strangely missing. Its disappearance was especially strange because the cabinet showed no signs of tampering.

Unaware that the original was missing, on February 17 Washington used the certified photostat in his motion for a new hearing. The Surrogate granted his request and scheduled the hearing for the end of March. Although the clerk had told him of the decree's disappearance the day after certification, Landis never mentioned it to Washington, later explaining that he guessed the original was misplaced; surely it would soon be found. But he carefully refrained from inquiring from the clerk whether his guess was correct. But as MacLean reported in the *Bull* of April 1, 1933:

> By February 28th Landis had apparently realized that this alleged loss was rather suspicious and so after about a half hour's hard work he found another paper in the same court files, which had on it a pencil notation signed "John Hammond Dew." The first document was apparently genuine except for the signature "John Hammond Dew," and also the second document except for the four-line pencil notation and the signature. These two papers were the only pieces of evidence of any substance which the claimants produced at this hearing.

The hearing before the Surrogate began at the end of March 1933 and lasted for four days. During his cross-examination by Harlan, Landis revealed the highly suspicious manner in which the two signatures were found. And, even more important, Harlan forced Landis to admit that his wife, who had assisted in his research, had entered into an agreement with Mary Dew Ambrose, one of the six claimants. In exchange for their genealogical services, the Landises would receive 50 percent of the amount she recovered from Ella's estate.

The signatures themselves were submitted to Elbridge W. Stein, the Proponents' expert on questioned documents. He was a highly experienced man, known to Foley from his testimony in prior Surrogate Court cases, with exceptional credentials as an expert. He had enlarged the documents 2½ times and demonstrated his findings to the court, using stereoscopes and other optical instruments. The enlargement showed the lines of the first signature to be irregular and variable in width—a sign that it was a tracing. Where it crossed a fold of the paper, the ink had gone through, as it would not have done on an original. The second signature, written in pencil, had made an impression on the back of the paper, which would have long since disappeared if it dated before 1850. Stein concluded that both signatures were tracings, neither being the genuine signature of John Hammond Dew.

As Stein wrote in a privately printed pamphlet after the Wendel estate was closed:

> Some of the essential documents offered in court by a few of the other rejected claimants were in the form of photostatic reproductions. It was claimed that the originals of these important documents, some of which were public records, had been lost after a photostatic copy had been made. This action is generally evidence that because of outright forgery, or material alteration, the original document would not bear a searching scientific examination. A photostatic reproduction of a document tends to cover up some of the most significant indications of fraud, therefore, an

> alleged lost important document represented by a photostatic copy has now come to be a common form of attempted proof of a forged or altered document.

His testimony to this effect before Foley was totally convincing and formed a substantial part of Foley's findings that the documents were forgeries:

> I do not like to characterize in strong language my observations of what was done to attempt to overcome the effect of my previous decision. I do believe the story of Mr. Stein, the handwriting expert, in his opinion that someone went out deliberately, in a very clever, scheming fashion, to manufacture certain pieces of evidence in this case, to supply the missing evidence which I stressed in my original decision.

Not only were there forgeries, but the testimony of Landis was found by Foley to be not worthy of belief. For any expert whose compensation depends on the outcome of the litigation is no longer impartial—his testimony is colored by his financial stake in the result. So for the second time, Foley dismissed the six Dew sisters' claim.

Incredibly Washington still persisted, still hoping his clients would win the Wendel sweepstakes. Although Landis, his expert, had been discredited and the discoveries branded as forgeries, he informed the court that he wanted another hearing. In May 1933, Washington said in an affidavit: ". . . [I] instructed Mr. Landis to continue in his search for evidence respecting John Hammond Dew." Landis again produced a "miracle" in the form of several new discoveries.

Over the protests of Harlan and Hays, Foley agreed to reopen the case, for fear of creating reversible error. The new hearing date was set for June 1933.

Fifty years later, Charles MacLean vividly remembers receiving the new documents and taking them home to study over the weekend. Not surprisingly, part of one document was missing, the back of a legal summons in an action. But the pencil impression of *John Hammond Dew* from the missing part had come through the photostat of the front of the summons. Using his wife's compact, MacLean read the mirror writing and pointed it out to Elbridge Stein. Stein emphatically concurred that the documents were fabrications and so testified before Foley.

The Surrogate held:

> In my opinion the two alleged newly discovered documents written in pencil, containing the name in one case and the alleged signature of "John Hammond Dew" in the other, are spurious and were recently fabricated to supply a grave defect of proof stressed in my original decision. . . . In it I pointed out that all the documents in the case showed that the grandfather of the claimants was John Howell Dew, and not John Hammond Dew, the uncle of Ella Wendel. It also plainly appears that a pencil was employed in these fabricated documents in order to avoid the more easily discoverable forgery, if pen and ink had been used. It is significant, also that the circumstances of their appearance and discovery are much similar to two other documents received on the second hearing in this matter and likewise found by me to be spurious. . . .
>
> I specifically hold that this alleged newly discovered evidence does not justify any modification or change in my previous determination that these claimants are not related to Ella Wendel, the decedent here.

And by now Foley had had *his* fill of the Dew sisters and their attorneys.

> In view of the persistent and unwarranted efforts of these claimants to inject themselves into this estate upon testimony and documentary proof supplied by a genealogical expert and other witnesses who have a contingent interest in the outcome of

> this litigation, counsel for the proponent is directed to submit the record in this case to the Grievance Committee of the Association of the Bar of the City of New York for appropriate action.

After a preliminary hearing, the Grievance Committee took no action against the Dews' attorneys. But the case was still not closed. One of the sisters later wrote to Hays, saying they had "fired" Washington and asking him to represent them. Hays replied that he was "astounded" by the letter. His firm had, at all three hearings, opposed their claim as fraudulent; his employee, Maslow, had worked with Robbins on the census records and the various tombstones to unearth evidence against their claim. Hays emphatically refused. At last, this was the end of the Tennessee Dews.

15. THOMAS PATRICK MORRIS: INITIAL SURROGATE'S COURT HEARINGS

"All of this may be a monstrous hoax—or it may be absolutely true."
SURROGATE FOLEY AT THE FIRST DAY'S HEARING

On July 26, 1932, seated before the carved figure of blindfolded Justice holding the scales, Foley began to hear the proof of Morris's claim. Room 503 of the Surrogate's Court was packed that day, with the lawyers involved and their clients and also with the public, roused by the extensive newspaper publicity of a potentially sensational hearing. And, of course, the newspaper and wire-service reporters were present to file even more provocative stories.

Wise and Martin appeared as counsel for Morris, and Harlan, Friendly, Root and Buckner of Root Clark represented the Proponents. Hays and Untermyer, aided by Schulman and Maslow, were there on behalf of their four fifth-degree claimants; although they lacked the financial resources to investigate Morris, they were confident that Root Clark would get his claim dismissed.

Still, it was an uneasy alliance. Once the lawyers were seated, Friendly noticed that Untermyer was trying to read his file over his shoulder. He recalls how offended he was at this rudeness and how he closed his file vehemently, making more noise than he intended. When Foley looked over inquiringly, Friendly apologized for the disturbance. Apparently Untermyer complained, for the next morning Root asked Friendly what had happened. As Friendly explained, Root began to laugh. "Forget it," he said. "It was the finest thing you could have done."

As the hearing began, Halstead and Elbridge Stein identified the authentic handwriting of John G. Then the protagonist of the drama was sworn, to tell his amazing story. He spoke in the simple language of an uneducated man with a thick Scottish brogue.

He was an unemployed house painter, he testified, and he suffered from angina. Born on January 3, 1880, in Dundee, Scotland, he was raised with eight other children by Peter and Margaret Morris, whom he had originally believed to be his parents. Peter Morris was a cobbler, and his family occupied an extremely humble home. After attending a Roman Catholic school in Dundee, Morris went to work at age fourteen in a jute mill and later a shipyard. From there he went to sea and then joined the Perth militia. He identified John G. from a photograph and a magazine cartoon and described his baggy, tweed clothes and his unusual shoes.

Q. When did you first meet John G. Wendel?
A. When I was about four or five years old.

Q. When did you next see him?
A. I seen him every other year or so . . . until I was sixteen years old. . . . He would come every other year for about three or four weeks.

When John G. came, Morris testified, "He picked me up and hugged and kissed me and let me play on his knee . . . and used to give me money." Asked to recall other details of the visits, Morris mentioned that the household seemed "flush of money" after John G.'s departure.

In 1901, five or six months after Morris's twenty-first birthday, John G. again visited Dundee. At that time, he gave Morris the copy of *Blockade* and also a watch and chain. When Morris asked him about the writing in the book, John G. had tears in his eyes. "Don't show that book to anyone," he said. "It is all the truth."

Morris told John G. that he had married and that his wife was expecting a baby. At first John G. was angry at not being told sooner, but then he calmed down. At this juncture the Surrogate asked Wise whether Morris claimed that the handwriting in *Blockade* was that of John G. Wise gave a most curious reply:

> I should state at this time, your Honor, in view of what you said, that my client does not claim that this is the handwriting of John G. Wendel, nor does he admit that it is not. He has no proof to offer on the subject.

Morris went on to say that he did not see John G. again until July 1906. At the time, he was a painter on the S.S. *Caledonia* of the Anchor Line and jumped ship to find a job in New York. On the very day he arrived, while making his way to Bay Ridge, Brooklyn, where friends of his wife lived, wholly by chance he ran into John G. in City Hall Park. John G. was "angry and scolded me for coming to the country without letting him know. After I told him about my foster-mother being dead, he calmed down. . . ." John G. asked if he still had the book, and Morris revealed it in the waistband of his pants. Then John G. took him to the train for Bay Ridge and handed him a $10 bill.

Morris became a housepainter in New York City and made no demands on John G. for money or a job. As he testified, until the wedding certificate was sent by Rose McAvan in early 1932, he really didn't believe he was John G.'s son. Still, the two met regularly by appointment in City Hall Park, and on each occasion John G. gave him a $10 or $20 bill. Once, John G. asked Morris if he had read the inscription in the book; Morris said that he had but questioned how John G. could really be his dad when Peter Morris was. John G. repeated, "It is all true. It is in the book. I am your dad." Nevertheless, Morris testified, he continued to doubt it because he thought "the old man was crazy."

One afternoon in early March 1907, John G. asked Morris, "How would you like to see your aunts?" He had never mentioned them before. He took Morris on a trolley to Thirty-ninth Street, where he rang the bell at 442. A maid opened the door and John G. went down a long corridor, leaving Morris standing in the entrance hall. "I heard loud voices." he related. It seemed to me that they had been quarreling." Soon, John G. came back, along with a very angry woman. He kept trying to placate her, saying, "Ella, be reasonable. This is my son, Thomas Patrick." Ella said, "Get out. You can't stay here. Take you and your brat and get out altogether."

On the sidewalk, Thomas Patrick asked John G. why Ella called him a brat. John G. replied that Ella didn't want to believe he had been married and widowed for twenty-five years. At this, Thomas Patrick said, "Are you all a pack of nuts?" John G. got very angry and lifted his arm as if to strike him but then, relenting, put his arm around Morris's neck and walked him back to the trolley. John G. then gave him a watch and chain he was wearing and a $20 bill. Morris claimed that the house did not display any signs of wealth—he had seen many better in Scotland. Morris later sold the watch in El Paso, Texas, on his way across the country; the chain he kept and put in evidence.

Without further word to John G., Morris headed West with a buddy, Bob Edwards, "riding the freights." Edwards's bag and his own, containing *Blockade,* were sent ahead by Wells Fargo to Kansas City. On their way, Morris testified, the two stopped in Pittsburgh on Sunday, Saint Patrick's Day, 1907, then went on to recover their luggage, which they rechecked to Albuquerque, New Mexico. Then someone told them there were jobs available in Clifton, Arizona, at the Arizona Copper Company. Arriving in Clifton, they had Wells Fargo retrieve the bags, and so Morris was reunited with *Blockade.*

It was in Clifton, in April, May, or June 1908, that Morris saw John G. for the last time, an encounter allegedly witnessed by one of his buddies, James Poole. Some directors of Arizona Copper from Edinburgh, Scotland (one of whom was named Lord Sterling) came to visit the plant, and John G. was one of the group; he had arrived in a private railroad car named *The Buffington.* Although Morris tried to avoid him, John G. discovered him and was "sort of angry" that Morris had left New York City without telling him. When Morris explained that it had been an impulse of the moment, John G. quieted down.

Then Morris questioned him further about his mother, Mary Ellen Devine. John G. related that, after their marriage in 1876, he had lived with her on Clinton Street in Brooklyn. When she became pregnant in 1879, she begged John G. to marry her in the Roman Catholic Church. He refused, so Mary Ellen ran off to Dundee, Scotland, to her friends, Peter and Margaret Morris. John G. followed her there, but since both were stubborn, neither yielded. Two weeks after Thomas Patrick was born, Mary Ellen disappeared. And so John G. "made arrangements with my foster parents to raise me and register me as their own."

Harlan's cross-examination of Morris, Judge Friendly recalls, was very gentle. The Root Clark strategy was to pin Morris down on the dates of the various events in his testimony; they were confident that they could prove, for any given date, the the events he described could not have happened. Very early on, Harlan had said:

> By the way, I want to be perfectly clear with you. If you do not understand anything I say, why, you tell me and I will make it clear to you. I do not want to mislead you in any way. I want my questions to be perfectly simple.

So Thomas Patrick felt assured that his questioner was his friend and not an enemy.

Year by year, with precise questioning, Harlan took him through his early life—the names and dates of birth of his foster siblings, his various addresses, the places in Dundee where he had worked and the ships on which he sailed as a crew member. It soon became clear to Harlan that the Morris testimony on dates and numbers was not reliable, that he was simply guessing. He first said his foster mother, Margaret Morris, died in 1893 and later changed that to 1904, while he was a painter on a ship going to Russia. He couldn't remember clearly the street addresses of his numerous residences in Dundee.

Morris was married in Dundee in October 1900—he forgot the exact date—to Sara Brodie, they lived one block from his foster parents. Then Morris went to sea and worked on various ships or in shipyards, although their names eluded him. In 1906 he left his wife and children to go to the United States, where he would get a job and send for them. His wife and his two daughters joined him in Clifton, Arizona, two years after his arrival. While in Clifton they had a son, Thomas Patrick, Jr. In 1912, sending his wife and children ahead, Morris came back to New York to seek a job. Even then, though frequently out of work and short of money, he never contacted John G.

After a quarrel, his wife ran off with her uncle, Charles Kelly, leaving her three children behind, and he never saw or heard from her again. Before Morris left New York, a neighbor had called his attention to a notice in the *Brooklyn Standard Union* newspaper of the death of his first wife, Sarah. He lived with his children at various places in Brooklyn until 1923, when he went to Florida, working as a house painter for various employers, There, he married one Mary Flynn, who had accompanied him from New York. He stayed in Florida until 1928, when he returned to New York. He had been unemployed practically ever since.

Why hadn't Morris come forward after John G.'s death in 1914, when the newspapers carried extensive stories of his wealth? Because he never bought or read newspapers, he said, and when he did pick one up on the subway or the trolley he read only the sports pages. He gave the same answer as to the newspaper publicity on the deaths of the other Wendels, Mary, Georgiana, and Rebecca Swope.

Now Harlan, having lulled Morris into a false sense of security, returned to John G.'s visits to Scotland to pin down the dates.

Morris originally testified, under Harlan's gentle questioning, the visits were generally in the summertime, in 1885, 1886, 1887, 1888, 1889, 1900, and 1901. When Harlan repeated these dates, Morris became uncertain and changed the list to 1885, 1886, 1887, 1890, 1892, 1894, 1896, and 1901. Harlan declined to ask a third time, for it was apparent that Morris would probably revise the list again. Then Harlan tried to establish the date when John G. gave Morris *Blockade* and the watch and chain. Morris fixed it precisely—the middle of June 1901—shortly before the birth of his daughter Frances, in July.

Morris continued, saying he was positive none of his foster brothers and sisters had ever seen John G. and he had never shown *Blockade* to any of them. Whenever required in documents to state the name of his father, he never gave the name of John G.

At this juncture, Harlan decided to shake up Morris, if he could. He told him that in June 1901 John G. was in New York, and he could produce numerous checks and letters to prove it. Morris replied, "I wouldn't know anything about that." Still friendly, Harlan said,

> You see I want to be fair with you so that you cannot say that I have not given you every chance, in taking up these years, to change the date if you want to. If you want to change the year 1901, do it, but do not come back and tell me I haven't given you a fair chance . . .

Morris held to the 1901 date. Then Harlan asked Morris if it surprised him that the Proponents could prove that John G. had never left the United States between 1879 and 1914, the year of his death. Morris very calmly said, "It certainly does."

Morris told his story with great simplicity, not pretending to be more educated or smart than he really was. Impressed by his manner, the newspaper reporters believed his story might be true, and at one point even Foley acknowledged the possibility. During the hearing, the *New York American* reported that the Residuary Charities had opened negotiations to buy Morris's claim, but no evidence of such an offer exists in the Root Clark files.

Morris's testimony and cross-examination were not given consecutively. Suffering from angina pectoris, he grew pale and strained from the tension of the witness stand. Periodically Foley would excuse him, filling the intervals with other witnesses.

One of them was Maslow, who testified on his correspondence with Rose McAvan and on the documents she sent him—the 1897 letter and envelope and the marriage certificate. Another was Helen Sandlass, the grandniece of the Wendel coachman Michael Lynch, now deceased; she thought that his signature as a witness to the will in *Blockade* looked genuine except for the capital *M*. And she created a momentary sensation for the newspapers when she testified:

> Uncle Michael once told me: "Don't ever be ashamed you're a Catholic, for John Wendel was ashamed of this wife and son because they were Catholics and he lost them both."

Later on, this statement, on motion of Harlan, was stricken from the record as hearsay.

And then there were the resemblance witnesses Wise produced. He had a magazine sketch in evidence, but only one photograph of John G., who had been extremely shy of publicity and successfully dodged photographers. Rose Camp, a chambermaid and laundress in the Wendel household, testified

Thomas Patrick did indeed look like John G., and one Thomas Mack concurred. Joseph Lundy, the son of Richard Lundy, the other witness to the will, stated that he saw a slight resemblance but then declined to identify definitely his father's signature in *Blockade*. A city planning engineer, John Hencken, who had seen John G. six or seven times, sought out Wise and offered to testify that he thought Morris's resemblance was "uncanny."

But the best testimony Wise offered came from Charles Edgar, who owned a stationery and cigar store in Thirty-ninth Street, between Fifth and Sixth avenues, that John G. had frequently patronized. He found the resemblance "very marked." He added that, on one occasion, he had remarked facetiously to John G., "You're very fortunate you are a bachelor." To this, John G. had replied, "You ought to see my big boy."

In rebuttal, Diaz and Shirk of the family office; Koss, the family lawyer, and Rabell, John G.'s lawyer after he quarreled with Koss, averred that they saw no resemblance at all between the two men. It was becoming clear the Morris claim would not be determined by resemblance testimony.

Now Harlan began to show some of the cards in his hand. The Wendel family had never thrown anything away. Just as there were 157 trunks at 442, along with mountains of letters, the family office at 175 Broadway preserved business records and documents going back to the 1860s. Even the attic there was crammed with them. Able persons—Diaz and Shirk, aided by young Root Clark associates—had dug through all of them to produce evidence for Harlan that could establish, once and for all, that Morris's story was a fabrication.

Diaz testified that he was thoroughly familiar with John G's handwriting and the writing in *Blockade* and the letter of April 6, 1897, was not genuine. He further testified that the Wendel family office was at 79 Maiden Lane until November 1,

1900, when it moved to 175 Broadway. His statement was nailed down by the introduction in evidence of the removal notice, preserved for thirty years, that had been posted on the door of 79 Maiden, with copies sent to all Wendel tenants and tradespeople. This was truly a blow in the solar plexus to Morris, since the letter found by Rose McAvan, dated April 6, 1897, allegedly from John G. gave his office address as 175 Broadway.

Then Diaz testified that John G. never left New York State, for Europe or anywhere else, from 1889 (when Diaz was first employed) until 1912. From the family office archives came three thousand or so cancelled checks, thirty-seven books of check stubs, several hundred bills in their original postmarked envelopes, and a large group of letters written by John G. from 1879 to 1901. The schedule they prepared from this mass of documents showed that there was never a period of more than two weeks when John G. hadn't conducted business in New York or Quogue.

Leslie H. Arps, then a young Root Clark associate and now a senior partner at Skadden, Arps, Slate, Meagher and Flom, still vividly recalls his amazement at the musty office at 175 Broadway, full of an endless supply of dusty papers. Under the supervision of Jack Merrill, he worked full-time for almost three months sorting through them with Diaz.

Yet in 1880, it took eight to twelve days to sail from the United States to Scotland, and in 1901, the journey took roughly a week. Adding this time to the three or four weeks Morris had testified John G.'s visit had lasted meant an absence from business of nearly two months—far greater than any gap between transactions. This was compelling evidence that the trips to Scotland were apocryphal, an inference fortified by the testimony of Koss that to his knowledge John G. didn't leave the United States from 1876 to 1907 and of Rabell, his successor as John G.'s lawyer, from 1907 until John G.'s death.

Rabell unintentionally supplied some comic relief to the seriousness of the hearings. Asked whether John G. was an educated man, he had replied, "Yes," volunteering that he had been a good speller also. The *New York American* described what ensued:

> At that, Raymond L. Wise, the claimant's attorney, tested the witness's own qualifications as a judge of orthography by asking him to spell "anoint." Rabell replied, confidently:
>
> "Onoint."
>
> When the mirth subsided, Wise tried him with "picnicking" and the witness spelled it this way:
>
> "Picnicying."
>
> With a relentless smile, Wise asked him to do what he could with "repellent" and Rabell did this:
>
> "R-E-P-E-L—"
>
> Perspiration beaded the witness's brow as he paused then plunged onward to destruction with:
>
> "L-A-N-T!"

As to the alleged first meeting of Morris and John G. in City Hall Park on July 23, 1906, the archives at 175 Broadway again disgorged documents showing that John G. was in Quogue on that date. And, regarding Morris's visit to 442 Fifth Avenue and his unpleasant meeting with Ella, Harlan asked, in cross examining Morris:

Q. Would you be surprised to learn that Miss Ella and all of her sisters sailed for Europe on Febuary 16, 1907, and were in Europe until the next June?

A. I would, sir.

Q. You would be very much surprised?
A. I would, sir.

Q. That does not change your recollection as to this conference?
A. No, sir.

Harlan proceeded to make good on his promised surprise. One Rolland Jenkins of the steamship line identified the passenger list of the S. S. *Cedric*, showing that the Wendel sisters had sailed on February 16. Letters that April from John G. to Ella in London were put in evidence. In fact, Diaz testified that not only was Ella away but he and Mrs. Diaz stayed with John G. at 442 from March to July 1907. He had never seen John G. come home with Morris.

As to the meeting in Clifton, Arizona, in 1908, the archives again showed that John G. was in Manhattan or Quogue from April through June. And using his diary, letters, bills, and other documents, Rabell could prove that John G. had been in New York the whole time, for he met with him on business four or five times per week.

And finally, Diaz, Koss, Shirk, and Rabell all testified that they knew John G. to be a bachelor. They cited not only his own statements on marriages of others but also produced a plethora of deeds, Surrogate's Court documents about his sisters, tax affidavits, etc., signed by John G. in which he stated that he was unmarried.

At this point, on August 4, 1932, the hearings were recessed to enable a commission to go to Scotland and Ireland to take testimony of additional witnesses bearing on Thomas Patrick's claim.

It is a tribute to Harlan's gentle demeanor that Morris did not regard him as a hated enemy. He foolishly viewed him as a sympathetic friend who was merely trying to get all the facts before the court—indeed, to allow Morris to strengthen his case, to enable Foley to decide he was the rightful heir. During the recess, when Root Clark associate Jack Merrill went to Wise's office to talk to a prospective witness, he met Morris there, who greeted him like a "long-lost friend." Merrill later reported to Harlan that Morris "made me wonder for a time whether I was on his side or against him."

Nor was Morris perceptive enough to realize that the web of facts Harlan was weaving would destroy his testimony and send him to jail. Just before the recess, he had told a *New York American* reporter:

> "When my rights are recognized legally and the money comes to me, I'll be thinking of my family and of others like myself—of people who are sick and poor and passed over by the world. I'll see that those who require medical and legal assistance and financial help get it as far as I'm able to, you may be sure of that."
>
> In speaking of the Wendel fortune he invariably said "when," never "if" he received it. Replying to my comment on his confidence, he explained:
>
> "R-R-R-Right is r-r-r-right and can't be denied forever-r-r! Over in Scotland we have a saying that truth crushed to earth will rise again, and I think it holds good in America, too."

16. THOMAS PATRICK MORRIS: RECESS BETWEEN HEARINGS

"Our success in destroying Morris' fantastic story . . . was the result of a number of factors—funds adequate for thorough investigation, good luck, hard work and the future Justice's [Harlan's] ability at organization and skill in cross-examination."

JUDGE HENRY J. FRIENDLY, 85
HARVARD LAW REVIEW 383 (1971)

Even before the first hearing ended, Harlan was directing the investigation that would be required during the recess. A.

Goodwin "Goodie" Cooke, an associate in the Root Clark Paris office, was asked to go to Dundee to interview Rose and James McAvan, the discoverers of the 1897 letter and the marriage certificate, and Mary Morris McLean, another sister of Thomas Patrick. He was also to go to Edinburgh to get birth, marriage, and death certificates for the Morris family, and most importantly, to try to get some evidence of the existence of Mary Ellen Devine. In preparing memoranda for Cooke's guidance, Merrill added a personal note:

> Please remember that among the beneficiaries of the will there are several Methodist institutions, so that your whiskey bills had better be charged to stenography.

Upon interviewing the McAvans and Mary Morris McLean, Cooke found their stories "surprisingly convincing." All three were very poor and ignorant, he stated, too simple-minded to have concocted the tale or to have learned it by rote from some master fabricator. Still, Cooke said, while the accounts were almost "too convenient and too neat, it will be hard to impeach the stories."

Harlan prepared an elaborate agenda of the investigation to be pursued in America, then left for Scotland, accompanied by Joseph P. Martin, one of Morris's lawyers, and George A. Shearer, from the Residuary Charities Committee. The prodigious research he had requested then commenced under the general supervision of Friendly, Merrill, and MacLean.

THE BLOCKADE OF PHALSBURG

If John G. had given this book to Thomas Patrick, he certainly chose a most inappropriate receptacle for the secret of his marriage to Mary Ellen and, more importantly, his will. The Bible or Shakespeare or Milton might have been more suitable for such momentous documents than this nondescript novel of

Napoleon's siege in 1814 of a town in Lorraine, after his retreat from Russia. For this reason alone, it seemed likely John G. never chose it. Maslow had found no paydirt in his inquiries at Scribners, so now John Melady, an investigator hired by Warren, began to check the secondhand bookstores in Brooklyn for reports of a customer seeking a book published before 1901 but not specifying a title. He had Morris's picture and finally, at Weber's Book Shop on Fulton Street, the two Weber brothers recognized it. They told him Morris had come into the store sometimes two or three times a week, occasionally purchasing cheap books at perhaps ten cents each. Then, around September 1931, they had sold a set of Erchmann-Chatrian novels, a series called Historical Romances of France, but the set proved one volume short. Although it could never be proven, a shrewd guess would be that Morris had pinched *Blockade*.

JAMES F. CALHOUN, THE MINISTER WHO MARRIED JOHN G. AND MARY ELLEN

James H. Simmonds, then a junior associate at Root Clark and now a senior partner of Simmonds, Coleburn and Towner in Arlington, Virginia, recalls spending a week checking the ancient records of one denomination after another, seeking the minister who married John G. and Mary Ellen Devine. He had no success. As a result, several hundred mimeographed letters on Root Clark letterhead were sent to every Protestant denomination—every seminary, every society, and every sect in the United States, the British Isles, and Ireland. They asked for information on the clergyman, not only under the spelling given on the marriage certificate but also such variants as "Calhon" and "Colquhon."

On the marriage certificate, after Calhoun's signature appeared the words *D.D., Pastor Castle Garden N Y*. One of the

Residuary Charities, the Methodist Church, noted almost immediately that this designation was unusual. The standard form would specify denomination and church, for example "Meth, St. Agnes Church" or "Lutheran, St. Barnabas Church." The inference of nongenuineness was clear.

Most of the hundreds of addresses of the Root Clark letter replied that there was no James F. Calhoun in their records of ministers. So Severance Johnson, whom Judge Friendly remembers as a fine investigator, was given the task of tracing all the Calhouns in the 1876 New York, Westchester, and New Jersey city directories. Another investigator, named McCool, was to search the New York City records for evidence of John G.'s marriage to Mary Ellen or of any other marriage performed by Calhoun.

Finally Johnson, in Albany, located a family who claimed a clergyman ancestor named James F. Calhoun. One quite reputable branch of the family described him as a nonordained street preacher, but they had never heard that he had married John G. and Mary Ellen. The other branch, Johnson reported, "was a rather nondescript bunch, whose members, dazzled by Wise's stories of fabulous wealth, have remarkably clear memories and would like to see their name in print—they remember vividly their great-grandfather married the pair and even more vividly that their father told them so."

By then it was abundantly clear that there was no actual James F. Calhoun.

WILLIAM E. SWIGERT AND LOUISE SCHMIDT, THE WITNESSES TO THE MARRIAGE

Severance Johnson was assigned to examine city directories for 1876 to determine whether these two persons actually existed. Then he approached all the Swigerts and Schmidts in the current directories for New York City and vicinity, inquiring whether they had ancestors with these first names who had lived near Castle Garden in 1876. At first, the responses seemed promising, but his interviews were to no avail. The two witnesses proved just as ephemeral as Reverend Calhoun. As Johnson would write to Harlan after the probate of the will was granted, "It is with pleasure that I recall those days of steeplechasing after will o' the wisp Calhouns, Swigerts and Schmidts."

CASTLE GARDEN, THE PLACE OF THE MARRIAGE

Castle Garden, the United States immigration station at the southern end of Manhattan, was the processing site for first- and second-class passengers from abroad; steerage passengers came through Ellis Island. Examining the records at Castle Garden, Johnson concluded that no minister had this pastorage or even regularly presided there. It was more of a turnstile for immigrants than a place where they might be detained, so the presence of a permanent minister was most unlikely.

MARY ELLEN DEVINE, JOHN G.'S "WIFE" AND THOMAS PATRICK'S "MOTHER"

If the minister and the witnesses to the marriage were elusive, the bride was even more so. Root Clark began the hunt with her marriage certificate, which stated she was of "Edinburgh, Scotland." A young associate, David R. "Ray" Shelton, checked the records of the United States Customs House from 1870 to 1876 to find evidence of her arrival from Scotland or Cork, Ireland, and then her return to Scotland shortly before the birth of Thomas Patrick on January 3, 1880. For six weeks, Shelton scanned the ship manifests—there were no indices of passengers' names—but failed to find any record of her arrival or departure. Then Root Clark hired two young women to complete the laborious search, now widened to include any record of John G.'s trip to Scotland in 1901 or 1902, when he presented Morris with *Blockade*. After some weeks, Harlan was satisfied that he could offer conclusive testimony refuting the transatlantic travels of Mary Ellen and John G.

In the meantime, Goodie Cooke had gone to Ireland to seek proof of Mary Ellen's existence. As he recounted in the *Bull* of January 14, 1933, he found himself searching for a needle—if one existed—in a haystack of women with the same name:

CROSSING AT SWANLIBAR

"No side of the exciting but unsuccessful claim of Thomas Patrick Morris against the estate of Ella Wendel has been less revealed to the public eye than the writer's trip through Ireland in search of traces of Mary Ellen Devine. . . . I feel that some small record of this eventful three days should be made, especially since none of the material discovered on that trip was put into evidence.

It became evident that if the mother of Thomas Patrick Morris was Mary Ellen Devine, she was probably in some way connected with the huge clan of Devines which sprang from Patrick Devine, a blacksmith of Killeshandra, Ireland. When the writer joined John Harlan in London, one of our first steps was to engage Walter Selby, ex-inspector of Scotland Yard. . . . Mr. Selby, accompanied by an Irish detective by the name of Stack, plunged into the wilds of Ireland and for nearly two weeks nothing was heard of him except letters saying that he was having a very hard time. It finally developed that he had obtained traces of five Mary Ellen Devines. Upon receipt of this startling and confusing intelligence the writer left St. Andrews, Scotland (chosen by that eminent golfer John Harlan as the headquarters for the Morris investigation), and traveled by night train, boat, and early morning train from Belfast, to Dublin. There he foregathered with Messrs. Selby and Stack who had acquired a slightly frantic look and a large batch of signed statements.

The next day we hired a singularly ramshackle touring car and proceeded hastily northward, stopping at Baillieborough to interview one of the ex-servants of the Wendel family; stopping at Cavan, the county seat of County Cavan, where we investigated many records and consulted the Rev. Bishop Dr. Finnegan as to the possibilities of further records; stopping at Killeshandra, a town of practically no size at all, where we talked about Mary Ellen Devines with all the oldest inhabitants, and finally closed the day by going through some records of 1860 which the writer discovered in the coalshed in back of the Killeshandra school house. The next day we proceeded northward, stopping at every mud hut on every wandering and forgotten road in the north of Ireland, everywhere finding voluble and enthusiastic farmers who were desperately willing to say anything which might bring a little money into the North of Ireland.

Not to make this reminiscence too long, suffice it to say that we obtained enough documentary evidence to convince us that none of the five Mary Ellen Devines could possibly have been the mother of Thomas Patrick Morris, hearsay evidence to the contrary notwithstanding. The most likely one was Mary Ellen Devine who married "The Wrecker Brady" in 1885, and later went to America. There must be fifty inhabitants of Killeshandra and Inneskillen who remember that wedding fine. "The Wrecker was a great one for the drink, and surely he was drunk for three days before the wedding. The Wrecker was a great one on St. Patrick's Day for leading the parade, on a fine white horse, with a green cloak, and him drunk as David's sow. Yes, and I would not put it past Ellen to have married John Windell [sic] and had a baby before she married the Wrecker. She was a hard case."

Inneskillen is in the North of Ireland, while Killeshandra is in the Free State. The main (so-called) road between the two crosses the border at Swanlibar. The border is closed at 10:00 o'clock at night and is generally passed after that hour by a little road that leads over behind the fields, or else by a bold dash at

> high speed. Neither of these methods suited our driver as we came to Swanlibar at 11:00 o'clock one night, with our lights entirely out of commission and a hard rain falling. It seemed easy enough, however, to find Jimmie Geoghan's Pub, and to gain admission to the same, although it was long after hours. Within the cheerful and beery precincts of Jimmie Geoghan's Pub we found the North of Ireland police and the Free State constabulary standing arm in arm with the customs officials of both Governments, drinking the excellent products of Mr. Guinness. No itemized traveling expense account exists which shows the exact number of stouts which the writer drank on that occasion, let alone the number of stouts he paid for. Suffice it to say that inside of an hour Messrs. Stack, Selby and Cooke were escorted over the border by the combined forces, swearing eternal friendship with both sides and promising on our sacred honors to come that way again. This is an obligation which the writer intends to keep.

And, finally, a Dundee solicitor was retained to visit The Crescent, where Thomas Patrick was supposedly born to Mary Ellen, who immediately thereafter disappeared. He interviewed the residents who had lived there in the 1880s, with entirely negative results. As he wrote to Harlan:

> To me it is incredible that the Claimant's story can be true. Here you have a crowded tenement house with no sort of privacy,—everyone knowing his or her neighbour's business. How could a strange woman have descended from the clouds, been delivered of a child in Morris's little house, and then deserted the child and vanished into thin air, without that tenement reverberating with a piece of gossip, the like of which the "wives" in that stair had never enjoyed before and could hardly expect ever to enjoy again! It is not to be thought that an incident like that could be concealed, or have failed to attract the most excited attention, and to have left not merely a lingering echo but an oft repeated and racy recollection. Yet, there is not so far a word of

anything untoward,—just the want of testimony one would expect in a neighbourhood accustomed, as part of the even tenor of life in "The Crescent", to the appearance at reasonable intervals of another little Morris,—a happening so ordinary as seems to be forgotten.

THE PRIVATE PULLMAN CAR, *THE BUFFINGTON*

Morris had testified in 1908 that John G. had come to Clifton, Arizona, in a private railroad car named *The Buffington.* Investigation of the Pullman company records show that *The Buffington* was not constructed until 1912, four years later. It was yet another chink in Morris's testimony

JOHN G. AS A DIRECTOR AND STOCKHOLDER OF ARIZONA COPPER COMPANY

Harlan obtained a deposition from the former secretary of the Scottish branch of Arizona Copper that John G. had never been a director or a stockholder of the firm. It went on to say that there was no "Lord Sterling" on the board, although there was a "Lord Salvesen" and that the company records made no mention whatever of John G. Finally, a group of Arizona Copper directors had visited Clifton in 1911, but not in the five-year period before that—hence, not in 1908 or 1909.

NEWSPAPER PUBLICITY OF THE DEATH OF JOHN G. AND HIS SISTERS

Robbins gathered newspaper accounts of the deaths of John G. and his sisters from the period after Morris returned from Clifton. In both New York City and Arizona newspapers, the stories received such treatment that they could hardly have escaped Morris's notice. Root Clark would present them to Foley to demonstrate the inherent falsehood of Morris's testimony.

THE "DEATH" OF SARAH BRODIE, MORRIS'S FIRST WIFE

Morris had testified that his wife Sarah Brodie had abandoned him and her children, and he produced a notice of her death. But in Scotland Harlan located her sister, who said that in fact, far from being dead, Sarah Brodie Morris was alive and well and living in California. Traced by Hugh Fullerton of San Francisco, one of the attorneys for the Barney claimants, Sarah Brodie stated that she had not deserted Morris—he had bodily thrown her out on the sidewalk. She was never divorced from Morris but lost track of him and had been trying to locate him and her children. She had never heard of or seen *Blockade*, or been told about John G., her husband's "father."

Who had inserted her death notice in the *Brooklyn Standard Union* of September 21, 1915? Suspicion naturally fell on Morris, for that publication was a lot less expensive than a divorce. Armed with a picture of the claimant, Robbins went to the newpaper office but was unable to find the original text of the notice or anyone who recognized the picture. Still, Morris couldn't have believed her dead, Sarah Brodie affirmed, for she had visited him and her children, en route from Charleston to Boston, after the date of the death notice.

JAMES POOLE, THE CLAIMANT'S "BUDDY" IN CLIFTON, ARIZONA

Friendly arranged through a large Los Angeles law firm, O'Melveny & Myers, to have an investigator, W. W. Hughes, go to Clifton to find James Poole and ascertain whether he would corroborate Morris's testimony on John G.'s trip to Arizona. Hughes hit paydirt. Poole didn't hear from Morris after 1912, when Morris returned to New York, but in the months before the first hearing he had received not one letter but two. At first he wouldn't show them to Hughes, though later he let him read them, and finally, with a good deal of buttering (and perhaps liquoring) up, Poole permitted Hughes to make photostats of them. They were to prove extremely useful at the resumed hearings.

EVIDENCE THAT MORRIS WOULD HAVE TO CHANGE CERTAIN DATES IN HIS TESTIMONY

Schwabe had been sent to Clifton, Arizona, to see Morris's employment records. He telegraphed Friendly that the records revealed that Morris worked there from March 7, 1808, to May 9, 1912. He had previously testified that he started work in 1907.

Meanwhile, in Scotland, Harlan obtained certified copies of Morris's marriage certificate and of the birth certificate of his first child, Frances. In questioning Morris, Harlan had carefully pinned him down to 1901, shortly before his daughter's birth, as the date John G. presented him with *Blockade* and the watch and chain. But now the incontrovertible evidence showed his marriage to have been in 1901 and Frances's birth in 1902. Harlan correctly predicted that Morris would revise his story.

In addition, Harlan had certified copies of the crew list of the S. S. *Caledonia*, showing that Morris had jumped ship in New York on June 14, 1907—not in 1906. Again, Harlan anticipated that Morris would change the date of his first meeting with John G. in City Hall Park.

To prepare for these revisions, Harlan told his office that all the meticulous research done to disprove the earlier dates should be repeated. So Shirk, Diaz, and their associates went back to the dusty archives to begin the whole laborious process again, this time dating the Dundee meeting with John G. in 1902, the City Hall Park meeting in 1907, Morris's visit to 442 in 1907, and John G.'s trip to Clifton, Arizona, in 1909.

CHARLES DIETOCH, THE THIRD WITNESS TO JOHN G.'S "WILL"

Of the three witnesses to the will, Lynch and Lundy were Wendel family servants. But who was Charles Dietoch? The address following his signature was the Libby Hotel, in New York City, at Thirty-ninth Street and Sixth Avenue, around the corner from 442. McCool, an ex-New York City policeman, found some evidence that Dietoch had been the bartender there. Given John G.'s aversion to drink, a bartender was surely an odd choice to act as his witness.

McCool discovered a Charles Dietoch who ran a speakeasy on Third Avenue near Fourteenth Street, and Friendly went there to interview him. He ordered a drink—and he still shudders at the memory of the vile bootleg whiskey. Deciding that while his allegiance to the Wendels was great, his allegiance to his stomach was greater, he waited until Dietoch turned his back and then dumped the whiskey in the spittoon. Dietoch kept insisting that Friendly buy him drinks and so eventually was persuaded to produce a sample signature. But because he kept drinking as fast as Friendly kept buying him whiskey, he was never sober enough to answer the questions—apart from denying unequivocally that he had witnessed the execution of the "will." Finally Judge Friendly gave up, reporting to Harlan that Dietoch was too much of a boozer to testify, especially on a point that the Proponents did not need to prove.

PEDIGREE DECLARATIONS AS TO JOHN G.'S MARRIAGE AND THAT THOMAS PATRICK WAS HIS SON

Michael Lynch and other witnesses at the original hearing had testified that John G. had made statements as to his marriage and his paternity of Morris; Edgar, the stationer, and others had given similar testimony. It was clear that from the depositions in Scotland that further testimony would be offered, now from the deathbed declarations of Margaret Morris, Thomas Patrick's foster mother.

It was urgent that a memorandum of law be prepared for submission to Foley delineating the law on the admissibility of such declarations. V. Henry Rothschild II had prepared what Judge Friendly remembers as a "brilliant, complete memorandum" But it ran 110 pages, clearly more than Foley could be expected to read. Friendly recalls Rothschild's anguish when it was abridged to 15 pages to make it more manageable for Foley. Still, more documents surfaced, more statements were collected. The dusty cartons of the Root Clark files contain a mass of other material unearthed during the recess between the Morris hearings. For example, Florida attorneys did a thorough investigation of Morris's second marriage, and his employment record there. Robbins investigated all of the places in Brooklyn where Morris lived before and after his trip to Clifton, Arizona, getting statements from landlords, neighbors, employers, etc. His children were investigated, and so were his friends, and even the meager romantic life of John G. Ray Shelton remembers sorting through boxes of Christmas cards and elaborate Valentines stored at 442. Severance Johnson investigated the witness Charles Edgar, who ran the stationery store. Every lead was pursued, every scrap of information investigated—producing far more evidence than the Proponents could ever use.

From Morris's testimony, Harlan had selected twenty-three points to investigate and to refute. As a result of the research, Judge Friendly remembers, "I was able to establish that Morris had lied no fewer than twenty-one times. When I reported my success, Harlan, undaunted by my exuberance and his own achievements in Scotland, suggested that we should concentrate on the remaining two points. Although this proved unsuccessful, his insistence was an impressive demonstration of thoroughness, his urge for excellence."

17. THOMAS PATRICK MORRIS: THE MARRIAGE CERTIFICATE OF JOHN G. AND MARY ELLEN DEVINE

"The testimony of Mr. (Elbridge) Stein, the expert on questioned documents, was particularly convincing upon this phase of the case."
SURROGATE FOLEY, DISMISSING MORRIS'S CLAIM

The marriage certificate Rose McAvan found in 1932, having presumably lain in Peter Morris's cobbler's box for more than fifty years, would be offered in evidence as an "ancient document." Such documents, if their age can be verified, are presumed valid by the courts, for the signatories who could verify their authenticity are long dead. Mary Ellen and John G. had a ring certificate, so called because of its illustrations. A bride and groom were encircled in a wedding ring in the upper left-hand corner bordered by turtle doves, across from a church steeple on the right; above the printed words *were united* appeared clasped male and female hands.

On first examination, Root Clark had no clue as to the marriage certificate's origin. Merrill had sent to Cooke, before he left Paris, a photostatic copy and asked him to inquire at as many Scottish stationers as he could visit whether they had a similar form of certificate. His assumption was that the McAvans had bought and filled in the forged certificate in Scotland.

Then came a stroke of luck mentioned by Judge Friendly. It goes to prove that Napoleon's dictum about good generals applies equally to good lawyers. Napoleon repeatedly said he didn't want "good generals," he wanted "good, lucky generals," because luck was part of a man's character and personality. One day as Harlan and Friendly sat in the Root Clark library, at a long table strewn with documents relating to Morris, Charlie Halstead, of Thompson, Koss and Warren, dropped by on an unrelated legal errand. Spying the marriage certificate, he said, "That is just like the certificate in our family Bible at home." With these fateful words the unraveling of the puzzle began. Judge Friendly recalls the excitement that Halstead's announcement caused at Root Clark.

The next day Halstead brought his family Bible, which contained a similar but subtly different certificate. Friendly asked the attorneys for all the Residuary Charities to examine all available family Bibles, and Drew University searched all

This Certifies
That John A Wendel
of New York N.Y.
and Mary Ellen Devine
of Edinburgh Scotland
WERE UNITED
BY ME IN THE
BONDS of HOLY MATRIMONY
At Castle Garden on the 11th day of
June in the year of our Lord 1876
In Presence of
William C. [illegible]
Louis Schmidt
Signed
James [illegible] D.D.
Pastor Castle Garden N.Y.

The "Marriage Certificate" produced by Morris

the copies it possessed. It soon became clear that the certificate probably came from a "parallel column" Bible—one column showing the King James Version and the other the Revised Version of 1881.

The only two publishers of these Bibles were A. J. Holman and National Publishing Company, both of Philadelphia. Leo Rosen, then a Root Clark associate and thereafter a senior partner at Greenbaum, Wolff and Ernst, who was on detached service there in connection with some defaulted real estate mortgage bonds, was asked by Friendly to visit both publishers. He reported to Friendly that Holman was the publisher he wanted, for in National Publishing Bibles the wedding ring appeared on the *right-hand* side of the certificate. His findings were confirmed on a second visit by another Root Clark Associate, James H. Simmonds, who went to Philadelphia for this purpose.

At that point, Friendly traveled to Philadelphia himself, accompanied by the expert, Elbridge Stein, to meet with William K. Holman, the president of the company and a grandson of its founder. Judge Friendly remembers him as a "crusty little guy." When he was asked whether the certificate had been printed and circulated before 1876, he replied with a sharp "No." Questioned further, he insisted that he was positive and said that he would be willing to testify. For him, that ended the conversation, so, abruptly, he rose and left the room.

Still doubtful, Stein and Friendly agreed that they would collect many specimens of the certificates, printed at different dates, and call on Holman again. Judge Friendly remembers going to Warren, who held the pursestrings for the Proponents, and saying, "I want $500 to buy family Bibles." Warren was startled, but after Friendly explained, he said, "Spend whatever you need."

Buying Holman Bibles became a major Root Clark enterprise. Simmonds and Shelton both remember spending a week in secondhand bookstores, looking for copies to purchase. Friendly retained Schulte, a Second Avenue bookseller, to aid in the search, who placed an ad in *Publishers Weekly* offering cash for Bibles. As Judge Friendly recalls, "We sure bought a lot of them."

Wallace Bates of the Washington office was dispatched to the copyright office—clearly the Bible could not be copyrighted, but were the marriage certificates? The answer came back negative.

By then Root Clark had accumulated a goodly number of Holman Bibles, with handwritten inscriptions in the front, of presentation from one relative to another, showing them to have been printed from 1874 to 1923. Stein and Friendly then drove to Philadelphia to see Holman, with the back seat of the car full of Bibles.

They had made no appointment with Holman and he was out when they arrived. So they spread what Judge Friendly humorously called "our merchandise" on a long table, in what Stein believed to be the chronological order from 1874 to 1923. When Holman returned and Stein showed Holman the increasing deterioration of the plate from which the eight-color certificate had been printed, the publisher became very interested. After Friendly explained the facts in the Morris case and that "the Proponents were prepared to pay him for his time," Holman grew fascinated with the proof of forgery and was eager to testify.

From his basement Holman produced orders for the various printings of the Bible, each with a specimen of its marriage certificate attached. Stein inspected these carefully and made an appointment to return to examine them with his equipment. By then, Stein had determined that the marriage certificate in fact had been torn from a Bible and its left-hand side trimmed to eliminate the ragged edge, for it was imperfectly cut, with the left-hand side a fraction of a millimeter away from being truly parallel with the right-hand side of the page.

The date on the certificate had been very skillfully altered. The original provided two digits for the century, followed by space to write in the year. Stein was prepared to testify that the *8* appearing on the "1876" certificate had been converted from a *9*.

When Stein finished his research and fully explained it to Friendly, Root Clark was convinced that this testimony would be the most dramatic in the resumed hearings and would convince Foley that the Morris claim was based on forged documents.

18. THOMAS PATRICK MORRIS: HIS CLAIM DISMISSED

The entire record points with overwhelming force to the following conclusions: That no marriage ever took place between John G. Wendel and Mary Ellen Devine; that Thomas Patrick Morris is not the son of John G. Wendel; that Thomas Patrick Morris is not the lawful nephew of Ella Wendel, the decedent here; that he is not a person interested in this estate because he is not a next of kin or heir at law of Ella Wendel."

SURROGATE FOLEY'S DECISION

The hearings on Morris' claim were resumed before Foley on November 15, 1932. Harlan began by putting into evidence

Morris's marriage certificate, the birth certificate of his first-born daughter, Frances, and the records of the S. S. *Caledonia* showing he had jumped ship in New York City in 1907. As Harlan had predicted, Morris changed his testimony on all the important years, offering the excuse that his memory for dates was poor.

But Harlan was prepared. When Morris redated the presentation of *Blockade* to 1902 the lawyer was quick to put the obvious, embarrassing question:

Q. Did Mr. Wendel by any chance ever happen to explain to you * * * how it had happened that he wrote [the letter and will] * * * in March 1901 * * * and then waited fourteen or fifteen months to present it to you?
A. Never spoke about it at all
Q. You never asked about it?
A. No sir.

It was the first of many. Morris had originally testified that the *Caledonia* had landed in New York on a Sunday, and that the next day he had deserted and encountered John G. in City Hall Park. But the landing date in 1907 did not fall on a Sunday—Morris had no explanation for Harlan. Similarly, Morris had claimed that, when hoboing in 1907, he had been in Pittsburgh on St. Patrick's Day, which was a Sunday. But in 1908 St. Patrick's Day came on a Tuesday—again, Morris could not account for the discrepancy.

Next Harlan presented certified birth certificates of all ten children of Peter and Margaret Morris. Their birthdates were:

Mary	November	1864
Helen Elizabeth	February	1867
Patrick	August	1869
Margaret	August	1872
Peter (*died in infancy*)	August	1874

Peter O'Connell	July	1875
Rose Ann	January	1878
Thomas Patrick (*the claimant*)	January	1880
Martha	January	1883
Bernard	November	1884

To eliminate Thomas Patrick as one of their children, Harlan pointed out, would leave an exceptional and unnatural gap of five years beteen Rose Ann and Martha.

Then Harlan again was able to show that luck was part of a good lawyer's character and personality. As most lawyers would in a case involving the credibility of the claimant, Wise had asked Morris at the initial hearing if he had ever been arrested or charged with a crime. Morris replied that he had not, but Harlan didn't take anything he said for granted. The Root Clark investigators ferreted out that, in 1914, Morris had been convicted in Brooklyn Special Sessions Court of compounding a felony. Assaulted by one John Bennett in a quarrel over a woman, he had filed charges against Bennett, who paid him $50 to drop the case. When the $50 came to the attention of the authorities, Morris was prosecuted and served thirty days in jail. Foley cited this perjury in his decision as additional evidence that Morris was a liar.

Harlan then put in evidence the newspaper clippings on the deaths of John G. and of his sisters thereafter. Morris still maintained ignorance, despite the nationwide publicity. Harlan also charged Morris with placing the death notice for Sarah Brodie in the *Brooklyn Standard Union;* this, too, Morris stoutly denied.

Then came the evidence of the extensive and fruitless efforts to prove the existence of Mary Ellen Devine, of Reverend Calhoun, and of the Witnesses Swigert and Schmidt; along with the certification by the New York City Department of

Health that its files disclosed no confirmation of the marriage. And to fluster Morris further, Harlan produced a letter Morris had written to Rose McAvan. In it Morris had described the initial hearing, enclosing newspaper clippings, and asked her whether Margaret Morris had mentioned his birth to her local priest, Canon Turner—clearly an invitation for Rose again to "remember." Morris went on to say, "The lawyer for the estate tried his damndest to break me down and tie me down to dates, but I wouldn't be tied down." Harlan asked whether that passage related to him. "Yes," Morris replied, "and you did try your damndest, didn't you?" This production of a letter of which he didn't think Harlan had obtained a copy disconcerted Thomas Patrick.

At this point, the *Herald Tribune* reported, Morris's "brogue thickened in his excitement," as he asserted his desire to tell "the whole truth." Still Harlan pressed on, asking whether Morris had written to his "buddy" James Poole since he left Arizona in 1912. Morris replied, "No, sir." Then Harlan produced a photostat of his recent letter to Poole, reading excerpts describing in minute detail the Arizona meeting with John G. In the letter, Morris explained that he was eager to find someone to corroborate his "memories" and ended with the interesting suggestion that, should he inherit the Wendel fortune, "None of my friends will suffer if I can help it."

This gave Harlan the opening to ask Morris how he could remember so well incidents forty years before when he couldn't remember writing this letter three months before. Morris couldn't reply.

Now came the noon recess, and in Harlan's and Friendly's hearing, Morris told the press that "he was 'damned' if he knew how the estate got hold of his personal letters." Judge Friendly remembers that at lunch he and Harlan speculated on how Morris would handle the second letter to Poole. They decided he would deny writing it, and they proved to be correct. When a copy of the eight-page letter was produced, Morris, shaking his head in disbelief, again had to admit he had sent it. Judge Friendly maintains that these two letters to Poole and the Buffington Pullman car impressed Foley that Morris was a confirmed liar.

For his part, Wise continued to offer evidence of resemblance between Morris and John G.. He called in John G.'s tailor, a former Wendel secretary, a former servant at 442—and finally Deputy Sheriff Michael J. Shea, once a tenant in the Wendel properties—to testify to the strong likeness. Mary Gibbons, a former servant of the Wendels, after her resemblance testimony, on cross-examination was shown three photographs by Harlan. She identified one as John G., another as Morris, and the third as Morris "when he was young." Harlan then revealed that all three were photographs of Bernard Morris, Thomas Patrick's alleged foster brother. By now, the *Herald Tribune* reported, "The faces of the legal talent retained by the estate were wreathed in smiles."

Then Wise produced a sensation of his own—a sculptor named Julian Bowes, whose sculptures in several museums and private collections were based on principles of dynamic symmetry, once known to the ancient Greeks but forgotten since that time. As the *Herald Tribune* described it:

> With the curiosity of the crowded courtroom thus whetted, Mr. Bowes then supervised the unveiling of the bust, which was wrapped in brown paper. Not content with the artistic atmosphere, he switched off a light on the Surrogate's bench and ordered that the window shades to the rear be drawn. Then he removed the wrapping to disclose an inner covering of white tissue paper, which was also removed, exposing the bust to the expectant audience.
>
> Under questioning by Mr. Wise, Mr. Bowes explained that, although he never had seen John G. Wendel, the bust was a per-

fect likeness which he had modeled from two photographs of Mr. Wendel, one of which appeared in the *New York Tribune* in 1914 and the other in *McClure's* magazine in 1912.

"It is a three-dimensional rendering with mathematical precision of the two-dimensional proportions I got from the photographs," explained Mr. Bowes.

SURROGATE APPEARS PUZZLED

Surrogate Foley, who seemed puzzled at the testimony, inquired whether the principle of dynamic symmetry ever before had been introduced in a court or used for identification by the police. Mr. Bowes admitted that it had not . . .

Morris was then ordered to stand beside the bust. Then came the real surprise. Directed by Mr. Wise, under whose orders the bust had been created, Mr. Bowes removed first the derby hat, next the spectacles and finally the mustache. The sight was too much for the risibilities of the spectators. Laughter ensued, until the Surrogate, himself visibly amused, rapped for order. . . .

"EACH INDIVIDUAL LIKE AN ONION"

Surrogate Foley then directed the questioning once again to the method by which Mr. Bowes was enable to construct a bust in the likeness of someone whom he had never seen.

"Every individual has his own schematic theme just like an onion, a rose or a cabbage," said Mr. Bowes. "Just as inorganic life has a symmetry in rocks and crystals so has organic life a symmetry which is the result of the upward pull of growth and the downward pull of gravity."

Wise's final witnesses were Annie Gordon and Mack W. Sanger. Miss Gordon, a retired trained nurse, testified that, at some time between 1898 and 1903, she had spent three weeks at Irvington caring for John G., who was ill with pneumonia. She testified:

> He was very ill one morning about four o'clock and said he had something on his mind that he wanted to tell me. . . . His breath was very short and I asked him to rest, but later in the morning he told me that he was a married man and that he had a young son who was being brought up in Ireland by an Irish family. He said the son's name was Thomas Patrick Morris, but in reality he was his son.

Later during the same illness John G. had repeated this statement to two doctors and to another nurse, her sister, Clara Gordon—all three were now dead. She told Harlan she had come forth as a voluntary witness because her conscience would bother her if she hadn't.

Sanger, the assistant to the president of the Checker Cab Company, said he had known John G. around 1910. He testified that John G. told him he had a son and also confirmed the resemblance.

At this point, Wise rested his case. Harlan then unmuzzled his big guns to blow Morris out of the water. He began with the "corrected" date, 1902, when John G. had presented Morris with *Blockade*, again producing a mass of receipted bills, cancelled checks, checkbook stubs, letters, and other documentary evidence that John G. could not have left New York that June. He called Thomas E. Snook, an architect employed by the Wendels, to testify from notebooks, diaries, and bills that he met with John G. on three different occasions throughout that month. And there was John G.'s letter to Mary, written in June 1902, explaining that he had to remain in New York, keeping his nose to the grindstone, lest "our riches take wings."

This was buttressed by the testimony of Selden H. Hallock, owner of the Quogue House on Long Island. Hallock, a man in his seventies, with a bronzed face and a full head of white hair, showed from his registers and paid bills that John G. spent a major portion of every summer at his hotel, from 1877 to 1914, including June 1902. To his knowledge, John G had never left the United States, and he added that John G. had never mentioned having a son. Unable to refute Hallock's testimony, Wise committed the cardinal sin of asking a witness a question without a clear notion of the answer. Pointing to the Julian Bowes sculpture, he said,

Q. Isn't the bust like your old friend, John G.?
A. Not a damned bit.

Q. Don't you ordinarily wear glasses?
A. Yes.

Q. Why don't you put your glasses on?
A. I don't need glasses to see that.

Hallock also helped discount Morris's new date of 1907 for his City Hall Park meeting with John G. He testified that John G. had spent that period in Quogue, and Diaz's mass of documents showed the same.

As to the new date, the spring of 1908 instead of 1907, for the confrontation between John G. and Ella at 442, Diaz testified that Mary and Ella Wendel had gone to Europe in December 1907; Ella's letters to Rebecca from Europe were dated in January and February 1908. The ship's manifest of the *Rotterdam* showed they returned with Rebecca and her husband, who had joined them, on August 3 of that year.

Finally, the last revised date—"early summer, before July 1909"—for John G.'s trip to Clifton, Arizona, was discredited as well. The architect Snook's records showed numerous meetings with John G. during that time: five in March, three in April, three in May, and five in June. Hallock's books, too, and the family office records showed that at the time John G. had been running the business by letter from Quogue.

Now, on the seventh and final day of the hearing, it was time for Harlan to administer the coup de grâce, putting into evidence fourteen different Holman Bibles published between 1873 and 1923. Each was bound in heavy leather with brass corners and brass-hinged clasps, and averaged between ten and fifteen pounds in weight. As Judge Friendly recalls, "Wise guessed immediately what we were up to and whispered to me, 'The marriage certificate?' and I nodded." Then William K. Holman took the stand to describe how he printed Bibles and the records he kept as each edition went to press. Through him Harlan put into evidence cost-record cards for the printings of 1900, 1913, and 1923, with specimens of the marriage certificate for each edition attached.

At the lunch recess on the final day, while Harlan and the others went to their lunch club, Friendly stayed in the courtroom to review his files and make sure nothing to go into evidence had been overlooked. Judge Friendly said he had a premonition that Dietoch would show up to testify as the third witness to John G.'s "will." Although Dietoch was told to stay away unless summoned, sure enough, he appeared, accompanied by his custodian, McCool. Dietoch had already been drinking, despite the hour, and was somewhat incoherent, as usual. To avoid embarrassment, Friendly gave McCool $10, saying they both needed a drink. The two left the courtroom to search for one and, fortunately, didn't return.

When court resumed, Elbridge W. Stein took center stage. He was armed with enlarged stereoscopic photographs of the documents, and a stereoscope, which he placed before the Surrogate. Then, slowly and carefully, he presented his testimony, discrediting the documents one by one.

THE BLOCKADE LETTER AND WILL. Stein, with enlarged samples of John G.'s genuine writing, showed unequivocally that

John G. had not written the letter and the will; the forgers had not even attempted to imitate his script. Then Stein showed enlargements of authentic signatures of Michael Lynch and Richard Lundy, the witnesses, obtained from savings-bank records. Michael Lynch could write only his name and this very poorly; most of the time he signed with a cross. But his name appeared on the will in a skillful, modern script, so well executed that Lynch could never have written it. This lack of resemblance and high degree of skill, Stein testified, demonstrated quite clearly that the forgers of the will did not have a genuine signature of Lynch to use as a model. Since they could not secure any papers he had signed, they had perhaps assumed that the Proponents could not find any either.

The signature of Richard Lundy, on the other hand, bore some evidence of attempted imitation. But when the writing on the will was compared with Lundy's genuine signatures from around the same time, there were many significant differences, suggesting forgery. Stein testified with certainty that both witnesses' signatures were forged.

Moreover, the will and letter had supposedly been written on March 1, 1901. Stein pointed out to Foley certain places where the pen had cut into the paper, leaving scratches that were white, not yellowed with age like the rest of *Blockade*. Clearly, the writing had been done long after the book's 1900 publication.

THE 1897 LETTER FROM JOHN G. TO MARGARET MORRIS. Stein testified that this letter had been produced by the same hand that had written the letter and the will in *Blockade*. Furthermore, the dirt on the letter and the envelope was too evenly distributed to have been caused by handling or natural aging. Instead, Stein said, both had been rubbed and soiled deliberately so they would appear old; the rubbing had raised the fibers of the paper so that in places they overhung the ink lines. And finally the clean edge of the envelope, where the stamp and postmark were missing, showed that it had been torn recently.

THE MARRIAGE CERTIFICATE OF 1876. Stein had summoned the full force of his expertise in examining the marriage certificate. Some years later, in a privately printed booklet, he summarized the testimony he gave that day:

> This form of certificate was printed in eight colors, the eight original plates being wood cuts from which copper-faced printing plates were made. The script portion at the bottom of the certificate was set up from type and then an electrotype made for printing purposes. This part of the plate, which had become highly individualized by a development of many defects, contained the silent but eloquent evidence which caused the downfall of the claimant's main document.
>
> Starting with only the Marriage Certificate and the plate from which it was printed, it would seem to be a hopeless task to prove that the certificate was not printed until thirty-seven years after the date it bore. However, a careful study of the printing plate in conjunction with a comparison of the other certificates that had been printed from it during the years of its use, revealed that occasionally a letter on the plate was broken, then later a part of the printing face of another letter became so worn that it printed imperfectly. At another later, period, the lower part of the plate came loose from the main section and had to be refastened in a slightly different relative position and finally, a serious accident happened to the plate which left two deep furrows across the type.
>
> Each of these successive evidences of wear or accident fixed a time before which the disputed certificate could not have been printed because these identifying defects all appeared in the Morris certificate. Finally, it was possible to demonstrate by the combination of the individualities found alike in the plate and in the certificate that it had not been printed before 1913 and that it was printed between 1913 and 1923. A series of carefully ar-

> ranged and enlarged photographic illustrations showing the printings of 1900, 1913 and 1923 with the Morris certificate between 1913 and 1923 established conclusively that it was printed somewhere in between these dates and was a demonstration that it could not have been in existence in 1876.
>
> The printed script date had originally been intended for use in the "1900" century but the *9* had been carefully erased and the paper was then ingeniously torn directly through the erasure. Fragments of a figure *8* had also been very skillfully inserted in the erased area to give the deceptive appearance of the "1800" century. The testimony regarding the erasure and alteration in the date area was illustrated by greatly enlarged stereoscopic photographs showing depth or the third dimension. These photographs revealed unmistakably that there had been an erasure and also showed the extreme care with which the "9" had been removed, as well as the skillful attempt to change it to an *8*.

Stein's lengthy testimony and the prolonged stereoscopic viewing failed to hold Morris's interest. The *Herald Tribune* reported that he used the delay to take a short nap. Thus occupied, he did not hear the destruction of his claim and the opening of the doors of the penitentiary.

Both sides having rested, Harlan moved for an immediate dismissal of Morris's claim. Foley took a half-hour recess and then delivered his oral opinion, which was substantially the same as that printed in the official reports two months later. It was a performance that Judge Friendly characterized as "remarkable" in its comprehensive grasp and analysis of both the facts and the applicable law. After summarizing the facts, Foley decided as follows:

PEDIGREE DECLARATION. The Surrogate excluded testimony given by witnesses that John G. stated he was married or that Thomas Patrick was his son. This testimony, being clearly hearsay as to the words of John G., was admissible, he ruled, only (1) if John G. was dead, (2) if the words were spoken in advance of the litigation (so there would be no motive to distort the truth), and (3) if the witness was related by blood or marriage to John G. Under the third limitation, Michael Lynch's statement to his grandniece and the testimony of the nurse Annie Gordon, the stationer Charles Edgar, and the others would not be admissible. To hold otherwise, Foley concluded, would "open the door to fraud and uncertainties which should not be invited or encouraged."

RESEMBLANCE TESTIMONY. There had been witnesses for Morris who testified that he resembled John G. and witnesses for the Proponents who testified to the contrary. The Surrogate quoted from Shakespeare's *King John* (Act 1, Scene 1), in which Philip Faulconbridge, the bastard claimant to an inheritance from Sir Robert Faulconbridge, his supposed father, pleads to the King:

> But that I am as well begot, my liege . . .
> Compare our faces and be judge yourself
> If old Sir Robert did beget us both
> And were our father and this son like him.

Then Foley ruled that he would exclude all the resemblance testimony from his consideration, not only under the New York rules of evidence but also because it was valueless. At best such statements were mere opinion and, as John G. had died eighteen years before, the witnesses' memories were subject to the hazards of time. "Look-alike" newspaper stories, especially of doubles of famous historical persons, had been common, Foley said, and served to show why resemblance testimony was too dangerous to be permitted.

In disallowing the resemblance testimony, Foley referred

to the Tichborne peerage case in England—one that the newspapers repeatedly compared to the Morris hearings. That suit was brought by one Arthur Orton, claiming to be a long-lost son and heir to the vast Tichborne estate, which had been owned continuously by the family since two centuries before the Norman conquest. His lawsuit became the lengthiest case in the history of English law. It had lasted one year (with time out for the four-month-long summer vacation) and consumed 103 court days. As Foley had ruled in the Morris case, the Tichborne suit was decided not on resemblance testimony but on irrefutable fact and documentary proof that Orton was an impostor. The Surrogate could have added with pride that the Morris claim was tried in only ten court days. In closing, Foley held that the Julian Bowes sculpture had no evidentiary value whatever, since it was prepared for use at the hearings and lent itself to obvious abuse.

THE 1897 LETTER, THE WILL AND LETTER IN BLOCKADE, AND THE MARRIAGE CERTIFICATE. Foley found all four of these to be fabrications, citing Elbridge Stein's testimony as "particularly convincing." And the expert's opinion was fortified by the address of 175 Broadway for John G. in the 1897 letter, an address not established until 1900. Foley called the error "a slip which is typical . . . of even the most careful conspirators."

MORRIS'S TESTIMONY OF MEETINGS WITH JOHN G. Given the mass of documentary evidence, plus the credible testimony of witnesses, Foley found Morris's descriptions of the meetings in Scotland, New York City, and Clifton to be unworthy of belief.

MARY ELLEN DEVINE. "She floats like a wraith or a ghost across the drama of the trial." Foley said. "There is not a shred of evidence that she existed, much less that John G. ever associated with her."

CONSPIRATORS. "The Surrogate believed that Morris had help in concocting his claim. "The stake to be won [by Morris] was large and the circumstances strongly indicate he was not alone in this scheme. Plainly a person familiar with the law played an important part in the conspiracy."

DECISION. Finally, Foley signed an order striking Morris's appearance as a claimant.

At this juncture, Wise and Martin asked to be relieved of representing Morris further. Foley acceded to the request, adding that there was no evidence showing that they were parties to the fraud. He then ordered that the testimony and exhibits be transmitted to the District Attorney of New York County for the appropriate action. Morris was to suffer the same fate as Arthur Orton—the penitentiary.

So ended what Hays had told reporters was "the most interesting courtroom mystery of our time."

19.

THOMAS PATRICK MORRIS: RETURN TO OBSCURITY

Is there a Master Mind behind the Wendel Mystery?
NEW YORK WORLD TELEGRAM
JUNE 28, 1933

No one who heard Thomas Patrick testify was ever satisfied as to how he came by his weird story, or how, when item after item was shown to be false or forged, he was able to stick to it so simply and staunchly. After Foley dismissed his claim, Morris said to the press: "I told what I knew. What we never had we will never miss. The money made no one happy. For my part, I'm happier a poor man the rest of my days. I wouldn't go through it again for twice the millions."

Opinions as to his intellect varied. Judge Friendly thought that Morris was very shrewd and that he feigned bewilderment when lies were exposed, knowing he would only dig himself in deeper by departing from his memorized story. Charles MacLean thought him "a sad-looking little man, involved in something too big for him to handle." Will Maslow, who had the greatest contact of the three observers, felt that Morris was stupid. He was convinced the marriage certificate was concocted as an afterthought, in response to his letter asking Rose McAvan for other documentary evidence in their possession. But whatever Morris's capacities, he succeeded in satisfying Steinhardt of the Untermyer office, Maslow, and later Wise and Martin of his bona fides. Indeed, Martin was so confident of Morris's story that he resigned his position as an assistant district attorney to spend six weeks in Scotland with Harlan taking depositions.

Who was the mastermind behind the scheme? Clearly neither James nor Rose McAvan had the requisite intelligence or the physical means to perpetrate it. Foley was confident the master mind had a knowledge of the law, for his manufactured proofs showed that Morris was legitimate and so able to lay claim to John G.'s estate. The "will" which was prepared in proper form was witnessed by three persons. Then, too, the mastermind had an intimate knowledge of the Wendel family. Since only two photographs were ever published of John G., the "recluse of Fifth Avenue," only a close associate could have provided details on his appearance, down to has baggy tweed trousers and his shoes with gutta-percha soles. And inside knowledge was required to select Lynch and Lundy, deceased household employees, as the witnesses to John G.'s "will." Most observers felt that the mastermind had to be a former Wendel servant. Only such a person would know that Lynch and Lundy were dead (and therefore couldn't repudiate their signatures on the "will") or that Koss was the family lawyer. Suspicion fell on Samuel McKinney, a former butler sent to Sing Sing for stealing $25,000 worth of jewelry and bonds, but although Hewitt interviewed him, nothing could be proven.

One point that perplexed Hays was the mastermind's failure to provide witnesses to say they had seen Morris and John G. together. And Stein was puzzled by the obvious effort to trace the signature of Lundy, while no attempt had been made to approximate John G.'s authentic handwriting.

The grand jury also believed there was a mastermind. On December 21, 1932, a month after Foley had dismissed Morris's claim, it indicted him as "John Doe", along with Morris and James and Rose McAvan, on four counts of conspiracy to defraud the executors of Ella's estate. Attempting to find out who "John Doe" was, the District Attorney presumably offered Morris the chance for a lighter sentence if he would give the name of the mastermind and testify against him. Morris stoutly maintained there was no such person. And so, despite his heart trouble, the would-be son of John G. remained in Harlem Prison, unable to post $10,000 bail.

The trial began on May 19, 1933, in the Court of General Sessions in Manhattan before Judge Morris Koenig and a jury of twelve men. Assistant District Attorney Edward McGuire appeared for the People of the State of New York, and Bernard H. Sandler represented Morris. James and Rose McAvan remained safely in Scotland, were not represented by counsel, and were not convicted as co-conspirators.

Substantially all the witnesses in General Sessions had previously testified before Foley, and simply repeated their statements. There was one new witness on Morris's side, Dr.

Earl Hand, who testified he had acted as a nurse for John G. in 1899 or 1900, and John G. had confided in him that he had a son.

Believing Morris to be innocent, Sandler fought valiantly on his behalf—probably without pay, considering the fact that Morris couldn't make bail. He handled Koss very roughly. In answer to a question about the number of claimants in Ella's estate, Koss described Morris's claim as "one of the 2,303 weeded out." Sandler continued:

Q. It has not been weeded out.
A. The Surrogate has so decided.

At this point, Sandler shouted, "Morris was weeded out because you have the will of John G. Wendel."

"That is a false statement," replied Koss, turning pale and motioning the nurse to his side.

Judge Koenig interrupted: "Mr. Sandler, such an outragous declaration is uncalled for and not becoming a member of the bar."

Koss interjected in an angry tone, "It is absolutely false," then began to weep and was assisted from the stand by his nurse.

On June 16, 1933, after nineteen minutes of deliberation, the jury found Morris guilty. Judge Koenig sentenced him to thirty-three months in the penitentiary—a light sentence, considering the fourteen years that Arthur Orton, the Tichborne impostor, had been given. As Morris began serving his time on Riker's Island, Sandler stoutly labored to have the conviction overturned. Finally he was able to bring a motion for a new trial, based upon allegedly newly discovered evidence.

Several of the grounds were clearly frivolous, but one deserves mention. Since Mary Ellen Devine had been held to be "a wraith or ghost," it was in order to invent a new mother for Thomas Patrick. Sandler obtained an affidavit from Amanda Mathilda Little Frock, the daughter of Lewis James Little, an "herb doctor" and obstetrician in a rural, "hilly" country. He had told Amanda that he had delivered a child from a meretricious union between John G. and his sister, Mary, at 442 Fifth Avenue, and that the child was Thomas Patrick. "Some time after his birth," the child was given to a Scottish woman named Morris to rear as her own. Thus, Thomas Patrick was not only illegitimate but was born of incest. To conceal the incestuous union, the affidavit continued, John G. had "planted" the forged marriage certificate with Peter Morris, Thomas Patrick's foster father.

Morris could not inherit from John G. since he was not legitimate, but he could lay claim if Mary was his mother. Mary (1839–1922) had lived a quiet life, untouched by any scandal or notoriety. Now she was exhumed so that Thomas Patrick could inherit Ella's fortune after all.

Still, Dr. Little's statement of pedigree was inadmissible unless he was related to the Wendels. Amanda had prepared for that problem as well. Attached to her affidavit was a genealogical chart showing that one Marie Elizabeth Wendel was married to one Patrick Klein (German for "little"), the grandfather of Dr. Little.

Again, the ugly fact appeared. Root Clark was able to supply the district attorney with an affidavit, with photostatic copies of authenticated original documents, which proved that Marie Elizabeth Wendel had died at the age of eleven months.

So Morris did not get a new trial. He served twenty-four months of his sentence, with nine months off for good behavior. In August 1935, he returned to Brooklyn and the obscurity from which he had emerged four years before. While

Morris was incarcerated, Hays in his book tells that Mrs. Morris came to see him, proclaiming her husband's innocence and describing her own destitution. At this distance, it is difficult to understand why Hays could not give her money, as he was clearly inclined to do. Instead he felt obligated to tell Foley and get his blessing for the charity. But the Surrogate said, "Arthur, I cannot permit you to give her a nickel."

Morris thereafter died in poverty.

20. PREPARATION FOR THE WILL CONTEST

"Ella did not know a damn thing about the will. it was just a nuisance to her and she did not wish to be bothered with it."

ROBERT PETERSON
PRESIDENT OF TARRYTOWN NATIONAL BANK

Now that the claims of Morris and the six Tennessee Dew sisters had been dismissed, the focus of the case shifted again to Ella's will and to the four fifth-degree claimants who were questioning her testamentary capacity and the degree of influence by Koss. Both sides had been gathering evidence to fight this last issue, the heart of the legal battle. For Hays, Maslow had interviewed neighbors and tradespeople in Irvington and New York City, and he had collected a number of statements from former Wendel servants as well. These servants were clearly digruntled that Ella had not left them bequests, once they read the newspaper accounts of her great wealth. And they were even more disaffected when they recalled her meanness over wages and household expenditures. If Ella had been conscious of the size of her fortune and if she had cared about her will, perhaps she would have remembered them.

Most of the evidence gathered by Maslow was known to Root Clark. Emory Buckner's memorandum to the Residuary Charities reports that over two hundred witnesses were interviewed. Jack Merrill and Bob Fiske had visited all of the living persons whose names were disclosed in letters to and from Ella, all former servants, plus George Washington Hill, president of the American Tobacco Company and Ella's neighbor in Irvington. Fiske remembers vividly Ella's signs on the Wendel driveway there: NO AUTOMOBILES ALLOWED and on the screen door: DOORBELL IS BEHIND DOOR. WHERE DO YOU THINK IT WOULD BE? John Gray, now a senior partner at Dewey Ballantine, spent a week in a boardinghouse, along with Charlie Halstead, interviewing Ella's "poor, uneducated, hardworking neighbors" in Irvington. He remembers that when he questioned one couple as to Ella's competence, the woman replied that he "would not want to hear her answer." Gray also picked up more evidence, as if it were needed, of Ella's peculiar way of life, including a report that she used to carry handkerchiefs to wipe Tobey's rear end.

Friendly, too, interviewed Irvington neighbors, finding none who seemed useful for the Proponents, and also spoke at length with Annie Gavin. While Annie was devoted to Ella, Friendly felt she was an unstable person who would not be able to stand up to Untermyer's vigorous cross-examination. And under New York law, Annie could not testify on Ella's competence without renouncing her $25,000 legacy. While the Residuary Charities were willing to reimburse the loss, Untermyer would have made capital of the reimbursement.

As the researchers collected Ella's letters, Harlan assigned people to decipher and transcribe them. They were very strange letters indeed. Ella started writing in the upper left-hand corner of a page, continuing on a slant, to the lower right-hand corner; then, on the same page, she would begin again at the upper right-hand corner and proceed to the lower left-hand corner, writing across the first half of the letter. Obviously she could not, by her lights, afford a second sheet of paper. The Root Clark files contain an entire carton—seventeen volumes—of typewritten transcripts of Ella's letters covering the period from 1880 to 1931. Surely it had been a Herculean task to reproduce them.

The letters certainly did not fill Root Clark with confidence as to Ella's competence. A letter to Diaz on January 3, 1930, complained:

> Henry's [the houseman] bills have $6.30 for fares to Irvington and return and then again in December 6.30. Annie says the fare and return was $1.80. . . . He changed the electric bulbs in the chandelier at 442, who choached [sic] him to do it.

Although she had inherited $13 million from Rebecca's estate, she had far more important concerns. On February 1, 1931, she wrote to Diaz:

> Maybe there are some good tools left at Brambles [in Quogue] . . . such as a wide screwdriver with a black handle.

Nor would Rebecca's and Ella's diaries inspire confidence. Harlan had asked Rupert Warren to read them. Warren, later Vice-President and General Counsel of Trico Products in Buffalo, remembers spending more than two weeks on this chore. Rebecca and Ella both had noted the temperature and weather each day in Quogue and in Irvington—hardly diverting reading. Nothing he read, he reported to Harlan, would be useful to the Proponents.

And in Ella's diaries Friendly noted passages that would seem disastrous in establishing her competence—long entries about staying up until two in the morning sewing together old, worn-out blankets so the servants would not freeze to death. And Mrs. Diaz reported Ella had sat up all night mending bed sheets. Clearly, she had entirely lost touch with reality.

Beyond the issue of Ella's competence was the question of Koss's influence. Did the will reflect Ella's wishes, or those of Rebecca—or those of the lawyer himself? In October 1931, when the matter was before Judge Mack in the Federal court, the *New York Times* had reported:

> Referring to Miss Wendel's bequest of $12,000,000 to the Methodist Theological Seminary in Nankin [sic] China, Mr. Untermyer declared:
>
> "The chances are that she didn't know where Nanking was or how to spell it. She left large sums to Methodist foreign missions. She didn't go to church. In fact, she was down on the church. If we get a chance to contest this will we will show whose will it was. She had about as much to do with it as the man in the moon."

The first-year student at law school learns that if a will is to leave the lawyer preparing it anything beyond a memento in cash or property to show the affection in which he is held, the lawyer should decline to prepare the will and have another attorney handle it. Judge Friendly recalls his amazement: "Why did any lawyer in his senses draw a will leaving himself and Isabel such vast sums?" Surely he would realize that an attack on the will would be probable. Koss had probably drafted the will for free, knowing the Wendels and remembering that John G. didn't leave a will because he refused to pay for it.

But another lawyer would not have charged more than $200 for the work, and surely Koss could have justified the expense to Ella or even paid it from his own pocket.

From these interviews and from Ella's letters, it seemed that Ella's feelings toward Koss and his daughter were considerably blacker than those two had publicized.

Isabel had told the *New York Times:* "Ella, who might have had a child my age if she had married, grew very fond of me." But Annie reported that "Miss Ella thought Isabel vulgar, because she talked too loud and laughed at the same time." Ella called her "a big ox." And, regarding a bequest to Isabel of Ella's sterling silver tea set, the *Times* said that Ella had "mentioned it first in her will." Annie's version was rather different, claiming that Ella had said, "I left that to Isabel. I never use it and I didn't know what else to do with it."

THE IRVINGTON PROPERTY. In the summer of 1923, Ella told Annie that she wanted to leave Irvington to Stanley Shirk, who she hoped would live there. He had small children who would grow up in the house and then settle there after Shirk's death. But Ella said Koss had insisted that she leave it to Isabel, since Shirk "had plenty," according to Koss, and had been generously remembered in Rebecca's will. It is hard to see the relevance of this statement, if indeed Koss made it—or to imagine anything more damaging to probate.

And furthermore, Annie told MacLean, Ella had suggested an alternative—that her will leave Irvington to Isabel for life and thereafter to Shirk's eldest daughter. Koss said this could not be done. When Rebecca Swope visited Ella at Irvington in 1924 and Ella told her what Koss had said, Rebecca became angry, saying, "Of course it can be done" and that Ella should insist on Koss doing what *she* wanted, even if Koss was reluctant. Privately Rebecca said to Annie, "Wasn't that a tricky thing for Koss to tell Ella?" She confided that

Koss was "sore at Shirk" and seeking revenge because Shirk had not married Isabel. Annie's statement was confirmed by a letter from Rebecca dated August 23, 1923, telling her sister that she too had urged Koss to carry out her wishes in Irvington. Koss, however, successfully avoided the matter.

Nor, Annie said, was this the first time Koss had acted against the Wendels' wishes. Ella told Annie that he had persuaded her sister Mary to leave her Quogue property to his daughter, saying that Isabel had lived there summers for so long she had come to regard it as her home. Ella told Annie that in 1914, the night before John G. left for California, where he died, he had warned her against Koss. He urged her, if anything happened to him, never to "let Koss inside our door."

In many subsequent conversations, Ella repeated to Annie her unhappiness about the will, about leaving Irvington to Isabel, and about Koss's reluctance to change the provision.

DEVISE OF BROADWAY AND FIFTIETH STREET TO KOSS. Annie reported that Ella had wanted to sell this property, but Koss said it couldn't be sold while any of the Wendels were alive. This was a surprising—and suspect—judgment, for Rebecca and Ella were competent and a court would have given consent on behalf of Georgiana. So Koss wound up the owner of real estate appraised at $2,175,000. Koss had had Ella sign a letter stating her wishes as to this bequest, but since the letter was written by him its value in a contest was negligible.

ISABEL NAMED AN EXECUTRIX OF THE WILL. Ella told Annie that Koss had made this suggestion and she had gone along. One must wonder whether Koss told Ella that this inexperienced young woman would receive $750,000 in executrix's commissions while he and Shirk did the work.

The twenty-page memorandum that MacLean prepared on his interviews with Annie was replete with similar complaints. Ella often told Annie of her resentments when Koss arrogated authority to himself. She would say, "It is our money that's making them climb so high." "He was so poor that he couldn't pay his way through law school." "The man lived [then] on First Avenue, not on West End Avenue where our money took him to."

With this entire background, Friendly was convinced that the will contest should not be tried and that the Proponents should settle with Hays and Untermyer. Now and then, while the Morris case was monopolizing Friendly's time, Harlan had asked him about his preparation for the coming will contest. Judge Friendly recalls telling him it should be settled and, when they had breathing space, they would go over it in detail.

But it was not Harlan's way to wait and see—he planned to be ready for anything. He had dispatched associates to interview and research, and he now set Ray Shelton to another Herculean task. Shelton abstracted every case in the English-speaking world (not only the United States but also Great Britain and the Commonwealth) that had ever been tried on the issues of testamentary capacity and undue influence in a will contest. He had written a treatise of 352 pages dealing with every aspect of evidence that could arise in such a trial. Now, finally, Harlan felt prepared in case there were no settlement.

21. THE $2,125,000 SETTLEMENT

"Every heir of Ella—there were about sixty—received something—most of them a substantial sum—some of them a small fortune."
HAYS, *CITY LAWYER*

In early December 1932 Harlan and Friendly sat down to review the will contest which loomed on the horizon. The evidence both sides would introduce on Ella's competence to make a will, Friendly thought seemed weighted heavily on on the Hays-Untermyer side; and on the issue of Koss's undue influence, Friendly argued, the Proponents' case was even poorer.

And for the Residuary Charities the stakes had grown enormous. They had already bought up the claims of five of the nine established fifth-degree claimants. But what of the other four fifth-degree claimants if the will contest were lost? Should the 1923 will and codicils be knocked out, Ella's earlier wills would be meaningless. They left her estate to John G. and her sisters, if they survived her—but none did. So, four-ninths of her estate would go to the four Hays-Untermyer clients.

Harlan agreed. He felt the lead in settlement should be handled by Buckner, now recovered from his stroke, Both by talent and long experience, Buckner was a skilled negotiator. He would be a worthy adversary for the tough and artful Untermyer.

So Buckner, Harlan, and Friendly met at Root Clark with Warren and Hewitt and Shearer and Matthews for the Residuary Charities. The evidence on both sides and the pros and cons of settling were fully discussed.

After extended discussions among the lawyers of the five big Residuary Charities, Buckner was authorized to offer up to $6 million. The charities made the proviso that, if he could not settle for that amount, he was not to break off negotiations, but plead the necessity of further consultation.

They don't have any courses at law school to teach students how to settle lawsuits. Perhaps a pre-law course should include one in playing poker, for there are great similarities. You have a shrewd guess as to which cards your opponent (we will call Jones) holds. But what cards does Jones think you are holding? And, most important, what does Jones believe you think as to the cards he is holding in his hand? All of these factors enter into how you and Jones bet your hands.

In this type of negotiation neither side wants to be the first to broach the subject. Hays says in his book that Buckner did; while Buckner maintained the opposite. When Hays told Untermyer that a conference was arranged Untermyer was "choleric"—it was premature he said. In any event Buckner and Friendly went to Untermyer's Fifth Avenue apartment in mid-December 1932 to meet with him and Hays. When the lawyers arrived Untermyer was lying on a couch. Slightly ill, he wore a brocade dressing gown. The living room was full of orchids and other flowers from his greenhouses—Judge

Friendly recalled it looked like the smoking room of a Turkish Sultan.

Buckner began by accentuating the depressed real estate market, the heavy administrative expenses, and the large executors' commissions. According to Hays, he even added, "I'm even troubled about [getting paid] our fees." Buckner said he might be able to get a quarter of a million dollars for the Hays-Untermyer clients. When Untermyer called that preposterous, the conference broke up.

Hays and Buckner adjourned to Buckner's house for some drinks and further sparring, Hays saying the claimants' case was strong and Buckner stressing the hazards of litigation. Even if Hays won, he said, what with appeals thereafter, it would be many a year before Hays or his clients saw any money from Ella's estate. No more figures were mentioned, but Hays's instinct told him that, then and there, Buckner would go to a million to settle. Still, no agreement was reached.

Since Foley had informed the parties that the will contest should be heard promptly, Untermyer proceeded on December 27 and 28, 1932, to examine Warren at great length as a witness to Ella's execution of her will and codicils. Untermyer was arrogant and thorny as he demanded that Buckner produce Rebecca's will and Ella's prior will. Irritated, Buckner replied, "Do you demand them as a right or do you ask it as a favor, for if you demand them you can go to court." At first Untermyer accepted the challenge, but after an assistant whispered to him, he smiled. "I won't be stubborn," he said. "I'll ask them as a favor." Thereupon Buckner produced them. The examination was adjourned, to resume when Untermyer returned from his winter home in Palm Springs, California.

In the middle of January 1933 the settlement talks became serious. Hays was under great pressure from his four clients and their local attorneys. None of the clients, save the

Laura Oral Harrison heirs, were young, and all of them wanted the immediate enjoyment of their money. The local attorneys for each were just as eager for cash promptly. And while Hays never mentioned it in his book, Morris Shilensky remembers he wanted his fee percentage from the settlement as badly as his clients did; it would be the largest fee, by far, that the Hays firm had ever received. Maslow remembers that the Hays office was none too prosperous. Some time before the settlement, as an economy measure, the salaries of most of the Hays office personnel had been cut by 10 percent.

The stumbling block in the negotiations was Untermyer. He had set off for California in his private railroad car, stopping at various places along the way. Telegrams to the train went unanswered, either not received or simply ignored. After all, a man with four homes who employed sixty-two gardeners did not care if he received his fee now or later. His intractability exasperated Hays, but it would eventually reward him.

For the bets were growing steeper. Buckner officially offered $1 million, then $1.25 million, and then $1.5 million, and Hays was sorely tempted by each offer. But Untermyer, when he could be reached at all, would greet each figure with "Preposterous." On January 21, 1933, he wrote to Hays that the case was worth $4 million to $5 million. Hays disagreed and said they should settle for less.

Finally Hays realized he would have to go to the West Coast. There, with Untermyer in the same room, he would settle the matter with Buckner on the telephone. He did so, and Buckner made his "final" offer, $2 million—take it or leave it. Still Untermyer wasn't satisfied. He had Hays demand a "special senior counsel" fee of $250,000 earmarked for Untermyer alone. No rationale existed, other than cupidity, for a fee that neither co-counsel nor clients shared. At first Buckner demurred, then split it in half. A settlement of $2,125,000 was agreed upon in early February 1933. Considering that Buckner had been authorized to go to $6 million—and, if necessary, very likely more—he certainly proved to be a better poker player than Hays. If Untermyer had been free to do the negotiation alone, Buckner would have had a rougher poker game.

MacLean was assigned to prepare the settlement agreement under Harlan's supervision. Of its 139 printed pages, 23 constituted the basic agreement. The balance contained exhibits for each claimant and spouse to sign waiving rights to all properties owned by the Ella Wendel estate. A reserve of $200,000 was retained by the executors from the $2,125,000 until the claims of Thomas Patrick Morris and the six Tennessee Dew sisters were finally determined. An additional $350,000 was reserved to cover the federal and state income taxes that the successful fifth-degree claimants might be assessed. Both Hays-Untermyer and Root Clark had given opinions that the claimants owed no income taxes, but the issue was not resolved against the Internal Revenue Service until some years thereafter.

One of the successful claimants was an infant, Benjamin Harrison, the son of Laura Oral Harrison. The California Probate Court appointed a General Guardian, Edward Hazelton, to conserve his property. Foley might well have named Hazelton a special guardian to pass on the fairness of the settlement for the infant. But now, as Will Maslow had feared, Foley used his powers to grant a political favor to former Judge Henry W. Unger. As special guardian, Unger did substantially no work. Maslow wrote his forty-page report to Foley approving the settlement, and Unger received the princely fee of $10,000 for his services.

When the settlement agreement was finally hammered out to the satisfaction of all, it had to be circulated to various claimants for their signatures. The parties were dispersed across the United States, and Maslow still vividly remembers his journey. He was sent to Mississippi to get Rosa Dew Stansbury's signature on March 4, 1933—the day Franklin Roosevelt was first inaugurated. He heard on the radio that Roosevelt had closed all the banks. Luckily, Hays told him to draw extra money from petty cash, so he was not stranded there.

The agreement was fully executed on June 15, 1933, and approved by Foley on June 23. It was a date of special importance to Steinhardt, for he had resigned as a partner of the Untermyer firm as of July 1, to become the Ambassador to Sweden. If the settlement had not been consummated by that date, he would not have shared in the firm's fee.

In approving the settlement agreement, Foley patted himself on the back, but he certainly had the right to do so. He was gracious enough to credit the counsel as well for the speedy resolution of the case. As he told the *Herald Tribune:*

> In less than eleven months after [I decided] the order of the procedure of the issues, all preliminary questions were disposed of and the will contest could have been heard in October. . . . The entire course of procedure presents a model of expedition. It demonstrates that the law's delay may be avoided even in cases involving millions of dollars. . . .

The probate of Ella's will was decreed by Foley on June 29, 1933. As a condition of settlement, all the evidence on Ella's lack of capacity to make a will and on Koss's undue influence was to be incinerated. When Hays looked at Maslow's modest folder on these subjects, he exclaimed "This doesn't look like very much for the estate to pay two-plus million." So Maslow fattened up the folder with old telephone book pages and various Wendel documents.

Now it was time for Hays to cut up the settlement melon. Under the pooling agreement (Friendly's "parimutuel device"), the fifth-degree persons whose claims had been "determined" by Foley were to share their recovery with sixth-degree claimants whose claims had likewise been "determined." The trouble with the scheme was that Foley dismissed all, but did not "determine" any, of the sixth-degree claims. Neither Will Maslow nor Morris Shilensky can recall how Hays resolved this knotty problem, except that he unilaterally decided what fifty-five sixth-degree claimants were entitled to share—a decision that was to have consequences later on.

By now Hays had persuaded Untermyer to share his "special senior counsel" fee, on the ground that his firm had done most of the work. After deducting this from the settlement, he divided $1,262,000 among sixty-odd claimants. Individual shares varied from a high of $275,000 for Rosa Dew Stansbury to a low of $2,725 for one of the sixth-degree claimants. Local counsel for the various claimants received in the aggregate $266,000. The Hays and Untermyer firms each received $273,500. The $550,000 reserved for tax and other claims was distributed later on in similar proportions.

Will Maslow recalls that when Hays hired him, he promised him a bonus of $5,000 or $10,000 if the lawsuit was profitable. He still has a photostat of the check for $5,000, which Hays delivered with the statement that it couldn't be $10,000 because that would exceed the shares of some of the Hays partners. With his own share, Hays built a country home in Sands Point, Long Island.

22.

META WENDEL STRAUCH

"Only recently I was able to swallow my pride, admit I was illegitimate and entitled to inherit."
PETITION OF META STRAUCH

When Georgiana died at Bloomingdale Sanitarium on January 19, 1929, her $5 million estate was left to Ella and Rebecca, and ultimately wound up in Ella's estate. Through this connection, Ella's estate would be litigated for the last time. Meta's claim was not filed until May 1935, but it would prove as colorful as the others in attempting to defraud by forged documents and perjured testimony.

Meta claimed that Georgiana had become pregnant in Europe and taken refuge with her "relatives" in Bremen, Germany. There she gave birth to Meta on July 3, 1879—by sheer coincidence, precisely six months before the date Mary Ellen Devine allegedly gave birth to Thomas Patrick Morris. Georgiana allegedly visited her illegitimate daughter over the next

Georgiana, Ella's sister

twenty-nine years, and at various times John G., too, allegedly came to see his "niece."

The seeds of Meta's claim were sown in 1929, before Ella's death. She was a member of the Wendel family that originated in Bremen, Germany. Family legend had it that there were "rich Wendel relatives" in New York City with the names of "John Daniel" and "John Gottfried." John Lubben, a nephew of Meta Strauch and another Bremen Wendel, had come to America around 1925 and found work as a machinist in Brooklyn. In 1929 Lubben wrote to Koss three times, requesting an appointment with Ella. When Koss did not reply, Lubben then wrote to the Wendel sisters directly. Still, he received no answer. Finally he called in person at 442, but he was turned away by someone he described as an "old toothless woman servant."

On March 16, 1931, three days after Ella's death, John Lubben appeared at Koss's office and he had an interview with Warren. He stated that he was related to Ella but advanced no theory of relationship. He said that his cousin Emil Wendel, who had the family papers, was on the high seas, on the Standard Oil tanker *Polarine*, but would be in New York soon.

One of the Bremen Wendel ancestors was named Johann Heinrich Wendel. It was natural that Emil Wendel and Lubben would begin by seeking a relative of Ella Wendel who had a *Heinrich* in his name. Accordingly, at first they seized upon Ella Wende's great-uncle Juergen *Heinrich* Wilhelm Wendel, asserting that he was identical with their ancestor Johann *Heinrich* Wendel. So, on June 15, 1931, Lubben again called at the Koss office and this time he talked with Hewitt. He gave Hewitt a chart, which he said had been prepared by Emil Wendel, showing an alleged line of descent from Juergen Heinrich Wilhelm Wendel.

As Lubben attended to matters in New York, Emil Wendel embarked on May 22, 1928, for Germany to assemble additional "evidence" to substantiate a claim to Ella Wendel's estate. He arrived in Germany on the S. S. *Deutschland* in early June 1931, and must have very quickly found that the plan was doomed to failure. The records in Germany conclusively showed that Emil Wendel's ancestor Johann Heinrich was not identical with Juergen Heinrich Wilhelm, and, more important, they contained no evidence that Jeurgen Heinrich Wilhelm left any descendants.

Accordingly, Emil started a new line of attack, culminating in the assertion of a claim based upon an alleged relationship through Ella's great-great-uncle, Johann Christian Wendel of Havelberg, Germany. First he undertook a search of the records at the "Standesamt," or local registration office, at Bremen. He was assisted in his efforts by his cousin, Andreas Wendel.

After exhausting the possibilities in Bremen, Emil then set out for Dessau, birthplace of his great-great-grandfather, Johann August Wendel. As a result of the investigations at Bremen and Dessau, certificates carrying the Bremen Wendel line up to Johann August Wendel were obtained.

Up to this point, his work went smoothly, for judging by the genealogical records of Andreas Wendel, the family's line of ascent up to Johann August Wendel of Dessau was well known. But then came the task of completing the line of relationship beyond Johann August to Ella Wendel. According to the records at Dessau, the father of Johann August Wendel was Johann Heinrich Wendel, himself the son of one Heinrich Wendel, a brewer of Berlin. Very obviously, therefore, the trail led from Dessau to Berlin.

Had Emil chosen to confine his investigation to his true line of ancestry, the trail would have ended there. The baptismal record of Johann Henirich Wendel in Berlin, confirming his marriage record at Dessau, shows clearly that he was born to the brewer and his wife, Sophia Apitsch. But the truth hardly satisfied Emil.

On he went to Havelberg, the home of Johann Sebastian Wendel, the great-great-grandfather of Ella. At Havelberg, Emil called upon Pastor Otto Schulze, who as senior minister held the records of the St. Laurentius Church. Later Paster Schulze testified that Emil had come alone and had mentioned that his search was connected with the Wendel estate proceedings in New York. He remained in Pastor Schulze's house for about an hour, examining the parish register of births, marriages, and deaths from 1710 to 1752. In it was the record of the birth of Johann Christian Wendel (one of the sons of Johann Sebastian Wendel) on August 25, 1741. Two weeks later, Emil made a second visit to Havelberg, this time accompanied by a lawyer from Berlin.

Some time after Emil's visits to Havelberg, the Pastor noticed that the register had been altered. The name "Heinrich" had been added on the birth record of Johann Christian Wendel.

Meanwhile, the Bremen Wendels met at Bremen to hear the results of the genealogical investigation. Andreas Wendel reported on the line up to Johann August Wendel, and Emil covered the balance of the search. Emil produced no documents, merely stating to the gathering that all the records showing the relationship to the New York Wendels were now complete. So a committee was formed to solicit funds from various branches of the Bremen Wendel family, and the proceeds were turned over to Emil to further his efforts. While no claim was filed on behalf of Meta Wendel Strauch, she contributed 500 marks as a "loan" to enable Emil to return to New York.

Emil arrived there in September 1931. The following January, he informed Schwabe, the estate's German genealogist, that he and Lubben had changed their theory of relationship from an alleged line tracing through Juergen Heinrich Wilhelm Wendel to one tracing through John Christian Heinrich Wendel. Emil and John Lubben filed their bills of particulars in the Surrogate's Court, setting forth the new theory in May 1932. Around the same time some twenty-one other members of the Bremen Wendels filed similar bills of particulars, clearly based on Emil's investigations in Germany the summer before.

But, as Schwabe pointed out, the closest of the Bremen Wendels—assuming that the documents were genuine—could claim only in the eighth degree and the others in the ninth and tenth degrees. Surrogate Foley dismissed these twenty-three claims in August 1932, along with the other twenty-two hundred.

If Emil and Lubben couldn't get Ella's $36 million fortune, they would content themselves with the smaller fortune of Georgiana. At the time, Lubben told Schwabe that Georgiana had an illegitimate child living in Bremen, but didn't mention either the sex or the name of this child—presumably because, in 1932, he hadn't yet selected the person he would designate as illegitimate.

It took almost three years of maneuvering and manufacturing of documents and testimony before Emil, John Lubben, and the Bremen relatives were ready to put Meta Wendel Strauch forth as the "claimant"—one is tempted to say the "victim," for that is what she proved to be.

As with the claim of Thomas Patrick Morris, the estate would have to prove a negative—that Georgiana did not give birth to Meta Strauch fifty-five years earlier. Buckner and Harlan designated John E. F. Wood, then a young Root Clark associate, now a senior partner of Dewey Ballantine, as principal assistant. They also detailed Charlie Halstead of the Koss firm and retained Severance Johnson to help uncover the history of Georgiana and the evidence in the United States.

For the Bremen investigation, they engaged Fritz Strube, a practicing attorney in Bremen, and in June 1935, Wood and Schwabe sailed to meet him. Certain depositions were to be taken by George Castell, one of Meta's attorneys, and Harlan wanted to take others on behalf of the estate. Wood was to handle preparation for these depositions and also the interim investigative work. To preserve security in his cables, Wood had left behind at Root Clark an elaborate list of code words for each of the Bremen Wendels, each month, and each year from 1879 to 1910.

THE HAVELBERG CHURCH FORGERY

As Foley pointed out in his ruling on Morris, forgers are undone by small errors. John G.'s letter of 1897 to Margaret Morris, Thomas Patrick's foster mother, was exposed as a forgery because it used an address the office had not occupied until 1900. Emil Wendel made a similar small error when he added the "Heinrich" to Johann Christian Wendel's name in the birth register of 1741. He overlooked the fact—which Schwabe noted—that the church kept a separate ledger of deaths. The entry for Johann Christian's death showed no "Heinrich" in his name. A German handwriting expert took photos and stated in a deposition that the extra name was forged.

And even a prudent, careful forger, who had remembered to alter the ledger of deaths as well, could not have known that the Wendel family office had done some genealogical digging for John D. In 1846 he obtained a certificate of Johann Christian's birth in 1741. This certificate, provided by Heinzelmann, then the pastor of the Havelberg Church, did not show the name Heinrich.

Now the task remained to pin the forgery on Emil. Wood remembers that radio-telegraphy of pictures was a brand-new invention. He cabled Root Clark to obtain a photo of Emil from his former employer, Standard Oil. The next day, to his pleasure, the picture arrived in Bremen, where the pastor of the

Havelberg Church and his wife identified him as the person who had examined and altered the birth register in 1931.

OTTILIE BENSIEN, FORMER NURSE AND COMPANION TO GEORGIANA

Through Georgiana's correspondence in 1905 and 1906 with a friend, Mrs. Wehring of Bremen, Emil discovered the existence of Miss Ottilie Bensien, who was living in Germany. In August 1932 Emil wrote to her, implying that Georgiana had left an illegitimate child in Germany and holding out the hope of substantial money for her cooperation. At that point, Emil had not yet selected Meta Strauch to be that child, for his letter went on to say, "If this illegitimate child is alive, then . . . *he or she* is the only heir to the Wendel estate." He suggested the child's name was Flora—having been misled by Georgiana's reference to Mrs. Wehring's daughter, who had that name.

Miss Bensien's reply must have been unsatisfactory because Emil wrote again, this time less guardedly. It was a pity, he said, that Miss Bensien did not know whether or not Georgiana had borne a child. He asserted that Georgiana had lived in Germany from 1890 to 1902 and that she had been in love with both an Englishman and a man at Carlsbad; presumably the illegitimate child was the fruit of a union with one of them. Then he continued, in a highly suggestive way:

> Its a question of millions here, and it would be a pity if all went to the missionaries to China, and also to other people who are not related to her [Georgiana], and you can help, and you will certainly not regret it, for there is also money that belongs to you, and if something can be done, then there is still more that can be obtained for you. . . . The doctors' books are all that is needed, and you are in the profession so it is not so difficult. You speak of

> lawyers, all they want is only the case, and nothing else. . . . I have investigated the whole matter here, and no one knows the life of Georgiana. *Of the friends who knew her during her life about 1890, there is no one who can say no or say yes.* So now I hope that you understand what I mean in the matter."

These letters were clearly a mistake on Emil's part—a mistake revealed when they later came into the possession of Root Clark. Clearly Emil hadn't even determined the child's birthdate yet, since Meta was born in 1879, or her father's occupation, for Meta's petition states he was a German naval officer.

META STRAUCH, THE CLAIMANT

After all these efforts, the council of Wendels settled on Meta Strauch as the claimant. They close her, firstly, because she had a pitifully weak mental condition that, according to her doctor's deposition, made her an easy prey to illusions and suggestions. Secondly, her birth certificate bore the notation in German *allegedly legitimate,* which they hoped might be interpreted as illegitimate. In fact, Strube had unearthed documentary evidence that her father, Johann Herman Wendel, had left her mother, Meta Baarke Wendel, around the time of our Meta's birth; the later two children of Meta Baarke Wendel were clearly illegitimate, having been fathered by "Uncle Fritz," her husband's brother.

However, Meta's selection as prospective claimant was not disclosed to her for some time. She was kept in complete ignorance of her relatives' preparations. To begin with, Andreas Wendel had a talk with Meta Baarke Wendel, then over ninety years old, who then made the remarkable discovery that she was indeed *not* the mother of Meta Strauch.

In September 1933, Meta's sister, Gesine Lubben, consulted a Bremen attorney and then drafted an affidavit relating Georgiana's visit to Bremen in June 1879, with the birth of the claimant early in the following month. Gesine Lubben wrote out this affidavit in her own hand and had it copied. When it was completed, her mother, Meta Baarke Wendel, swore to it before a notary. Shortly thereafter, this affidavit was forwarded to John Lubben in New York.

With all the groundwork in place, Gesine Lubben then broke the news to her sister, Meta Strauch. On this occasion, Meta later stated in a deposition, Gesine Lubben said she knew she and her brothers and sisters did not "belong together at all" but that she did not know who Meta's father and mother were. Yet Meta herself testified later that Gesine's information came as a great shock, for up to that time she had had no suspicion that Meta Baarke Wendel was not her mother. Unwilling to believe Gesine, she went to her mother for confirmation and was told the same strange story. In her deposition Meta stated that all she knew about her alleged relationship to Georgiana Wendel came from Gesine Lubben and her mother.

Although Meta Strauch was thus informed of the story of her birth, she was excluded from the further plans entirely. Indeed, she was not consulted on whether any proceeding should be instituted, in her name, in the Surrogate's Court. The first intimation she received of her involvement in the suit came in a letter from Jacob Galerston, a New York lawyer, informing her that John Lubben had retained him to proceed in the matter of her claim, pointing out to her "the advisability of cooperating with all due diligence."

Both Meta and her husband told Andreas Wendel that they really did not want to open the question. They replied to Galerston that if he wanted to conduct this proceeding at his own expense, he could do it. Galerston then sent them a document that she described as an "employment contract," to be executed before the American consul.

The next step was the institution of a proceeding to change the Bremen public records so they would show the mother of Meta Strauch to be Georgiana Wendel rather than Meta Baarke Wendel. Gesine Lubben undertook this effort, according to her deposition, without mentioning it to Meta Strauch. Meta would later testify that even after the proceeding was well under way and her relatives were testifying, she did not even know that her mother was to give testimony.

Under the German statute governing the change of records, the tribunal would hear the "parties in interest," who could be summoned by publication. Although representatives of the estate of Georgiana were not notified, it was not feasible to close the proceedings without giving Meta Strauch a hearing. But when Meta's turn came, several days after Meta Baarke Wendel and Gesine Lubben had given their testimony, she never discussed the issue. She did not say that Georgiana Wendel was her mother, nor did she say that Meta Baarke Wendel was not her mother. For some reason the persons conducting the examination did not bring up those subjects at all. The only fact Meta stated was that as a young girl she was badly treated and insulted by her stepfather, "Uncle Fritz."

The difference between this testimony and the statements she made under oath in her petition, some eight months later, serves to illustrate the power of suggestion of the greedy relatives who surrounded her.

Once the degree was entered in Bremen amending the public records to show that Meta Strauch was the child of Georgiana Wendel, the next step was the preparation and filing of a petition in the Surrogate's Court. Written in English, this petition was meaningless to the claimant. Although "her" German attorney had made an affidavit that she had read a translation of the petition, Meta was very vague about it, unable later to recall any statements that appeared in this document.

After the filing of the petition Meta's participation in the case was as limited as it had been previously. The affair continued to be managed by the persons who had brought it into being. None of them troubled to discuss the case at all with the claimant. It was Andreas Wendel and Gesine Lubben who interviewed the witnesses and arranged for the attendance at the Bremen depositions. After the depositions had been going on for a full week, the claimant testified that she did not even know who the witnesses were.

While the claimant's relatives were handling the litigation in Germany, John Lubben was exercising a similar function in the United States. When he learned that Christian Wendel, a distant relative living in New York, had been in touch with representatives of Georgiana's estate, Lubben, who described himself as "the one in charge of everything," sent him the following letter of warning:

> I am sorry I have to send you a warning, I would request you to keep your mouth shut about matters which do not concern you for the time being. It seems you don't know that it is unlawful if somebody gives you 250,000 dollars of an estate. That's why I am asking you in your own interest to keep your mouth shut for at present you don't have the 250,000 dollars yet, and the party, who is going to give them to you, has not got them either up to now. I am fully informed about everything that is going on for I am in charge of everything. If everything should go through as expected, I shall see to it that you get all your money back. I am a superintendent in your neighborhood and am well informed.
>
> I would like to tell you that depositions of all the witnesses (23 in number) will be taken in Bremen before the American Consul on August 5th. Both sides will be represented.
>
> Please do me a favor, keep quiet.

Shortly before the beginning of the depositions in Bremen, Lubben wrote a letter of encouragement and advice to his mother, saying:

> In the meantime Mr. Castell has probably arrived with you in Bremen. . . . Now, dear Mother, I hope that everything will go all right with you on August 5th and that Grandma will stick to what she has deposed. That is all Mr. Castell hopes for. The other side will try to break Grandma down. I hope we will have good luck. I think if everything goes well you will come over right away. . . .
>
> I hope you have drummed it well into Grandma what she must say. Why did Meta go to Dr. Hyman? . . .
>
> Now, dear Mother, keep a good eye on Grandma and all witnesses so that everything will go well. Then you will have won. . . .

These letters make it perfectly clear that Meta Strauch's share in any cash proceeds of this proceeding would be as limited as her participation in the planning. If successful, John Lubben expected to be able to pay $250,000 to Christian Wendel to keep quiet and to be able to bring his mother to New York to live. His only reference to the claimant was the rather surprising question about why she had gone to see Dr. Hyman, the lawyer who had been employed to act in her name. Why, indeed? By his lights, it was not her lawsuit and she had no business injecting herself into it.

All of the foregoing was embodied in depositions taken by Harlan and Wood, with the aid of Fritz Strube. Questions were posed in English then translated into German, and the German answers translated into English. The proceedings were held before a German Notary, a person of considerably greater importance than an American notary public.

THE DOCUMENTARY EVIDENCE THAT META WAS NOT GEORGIANA'S DAUGHTER

In his usual, thorough way, Schwabe uncovered an uninterrupted succession of official documents in Bremen, covering a period of fifty years from her birth in 1879 to November 1933, in which Johann Hermann and Meta Baarke Wendel were stated to be Meta's parents or in which she acknowledged her membership in their family. The evidence included her birth certificate and baptismal records, a petition by her mother to have a guardian appointed for Meta, the claimant's statements on her marriage register, and her mother's application for support from the Poor Funds in Bremen.

EVIDENCE THAT GEORGIANA WAS NOT IN BREMEN

Again, from its inexhaustible supply, the Wendel family office produced a host of documents. Entries in Beckie's diary from April 22 to August 2, 1879, showed that "Georgie" was in Irvington or at 442 during the entire period in question. One entry on May 6, two months before Meta Strauch's alleged birth on July 3, stated Georgie's weight as 109 pounds. A letter from Beckie to Georgie, dated June 30, was clearly addressed to her in Irvington, where she was staying with Ella and Mary.

Rupert Warren was assigned to read Georgiana's diaries for the period she was allegedly pregnant. In July 1896, the time of her alleged first visit to Bremen, Georgie was in a sanitarium at Denville, New Jersey. Her stay there was confirmed by Father Joch, who managed the institution and by its register and books of account, and was corroborated by Georgie's check stubs. In April 1909, when she allegedly made her second visit to Bremen, Georgiana was mentally ill and under the constant care of a companion, a Miss Dickinson. Both her companion and Diaz testified that Georgiana did not leave 442 during the first four months of 1909.

Judge Friendly recalls that he was pressed into Wendel service by Harlan, "for old time's sake." He traveled to Great Barrington, Massachusetts, to interview William Geisse, an old family friend of the Wendels—indeed, Geisse was Georgiana's middle name. Vice-consul of the United States in Nuremberg, Germany, Geisse had come to the United States in April 1879 and stayed with the Wendels at 442 and Irvington before his return to Germany in June. Beckie mentioned his visit in her diary, which was not admissible as evidence. Friendly arrived armed with ships' manifests showing Geisse's arrival and departure, but was amazed when Geisse volunteered the dates of his arrival and departure from memory. Harlan and Friendly then took Geisse's deposition. Geisse testified that during his visit in 1879 Georgiana had been very much present and engaged in vigorous activities entirely unsuitable for a woman in the last stages of pregnancy.

HEARING BEFORE SURROGATE FOLEY

Two weeks before the hearing, Castell withdrew as counsel, obviously because he realized his clients were committing a fraud. The other lawyer for the Bremen Wendels, Jacob Galerston, told Foley he wanted to withdraw his client's claim and not to proceed further. But Harlan insisted that the case be heard. The claim had already cost Georgiana's estate many thousands of dollars, and if the Surrogate permitted its withdrawal, the claim might be refiled at some future date. He urged Foley to allow him to present his evidence so the matter could be settled. The Surrogate agreed.

After examining the evidence, Foley made a ruling that was a complete victory for Root Clark. He held that Meta Strauch was not the illegitimate child of Georgiana and that the claimant's testimony was perjurious. In his opinion, he remarked on Meta's reluctance until 1935 to come forward and admit she was illegitimate:

> The bar sinister was not unknown to her family and the assertion of the illegitimacy could not have disturbed the family pride for there were at least five illegitimates in two generations.

On this note, there had been an amusing episode in the research. Mr. Wood recalls that one woman came to the office of the Notary to sign her deposition. The Notary told Strube and Wood that she refused to sign it because it wasn't truthful. She had testified that she had four illegitimate children, but in fact she had five. Wood says they all laughed, then the Notary changed her testimony and she signed.

23.

ELLA'S ESTATE IS WOUND UP

"Would today's serious young lawyers have gotten such fun from all this? If one wants to rationalize, I suppose there was some element of public interest about the case. Surely it was better that Miss Wendel's vast estate should go to hospitals, institutions of learning, and other charities, even though there was almost no evidence she had ever taken an interest in them, than to distant relatives she had never known. And if something had to be paid to avoid a long and dubious battle over probate, it was better that this should go to genuine relatives than to fakers. I cannot say whether such public interest considerations occurred to John Harlan, although I doubt it. Certainly they did not to me. Our pleasure came from the gaudium certaminis, *the joy of battle, and from pride in a*

task well done. Today's young lawyers are missing something if they have lost this.
JUDGE HENRY J. FRIENDLY
85 *HARVARD LAW REVIEW* 384 (1971)

9-year-old black cow, blind in one eye and hip down, $50; 1918 Locomobile automobile, $50; 140 chickens, $154.13; 13 ducks, $13.
ACCOUNTING FILED BY ELLA'S TEMPORARY ADMINISTRATORS JANUARY 19, 1935

Ella's estate was not completely wound up until 1941. But the periodic accountings filed by Ella's temporary administrators, as well as those following probate of her will are of more than routine interest. Her case especially well illustrates the point that some settlements are not really settlements until after subsequent legal proceedings.

Koss died in October 1933, having made sure that Isabel, his sole heir, would never want. She was an executor of Rebecca Swope's $15 million, from which her commissions were over $400,000. She had inherited Irvington and 1 Beaver Street, appraised for estate tax purposes at $100,000 and $180,000, respectively—very modest appraisals, considering that a Standard Oil building stood on the Beaver Street property, with rent subject to renegotiation every ten years. Then, too, as Koss's heir, Isabel had inherited the property at Fiftieth Street and Broadway, appraised at $2,175,300, which Ella had bequeathed to him under her will. And finally there was her executor's commission from Ella's estate, which Warren's fairly shrewd estimate placed at roughly $742,000. Had the will contest not been settled, perhaps Surrogate Foley would have agreed with Untermyer that "it wasn't Ella's will but Koss's will."

The accounting for the estate covered more than six hundred pages. The attorneys' fees of Root Clark were $510,000—almost $3 million in current figures. Judge Friendly, who was not yet a partner and so not privy to fee matters, considered the fees extremely moderate given the quality and quantity of the work done and the results achieved. Thompson, Koss, and Warren alone charged over $1 million, which fortifies Judge Friendly's observation.

The Hays-Untermyer pooling arrangement and the dubious special senior counsel fee provoked a lawsuit in the late 1930s. In May 1933 Hays had asked his four clients—Rosa Dew Stansbury, Grace MacQuarrie, Hattie Barney Simmons, and the estate of Laura Oral Harrison (with four heirs)—to confirm the settlement agreement then being executed and the division of the proceeds. Under the pooling agreement, each party was to pay 33⅓ percent of its recovery as counsel fees, but the three Barney fifth-degree claimants, who were the last to join the pool, had agreed to pay 38 percent. There was no rationale for the Barney claimants to have paid higher fees than the various sixth-, seventh- and lesser-degree claimants; they should have paid less. The letter Hays wrote to confirm the settlement mentioned the 38 percent and the special senior counsel fee, but not the additional fees that Hays-Untermyer expected for handling the tax questions, for which $350,000 was held in reserve.

So, in 1938, the Harrison estate heirs sued, on the grounds that the sixth-degree heirs had no right to any part of the settlement proceeds, since the Surrogate had dismissed their claims, and that the special counsel fee should have been divided among the fifth-degree heirs, since Hays-Untermyer had already taken 38 percent. The litigation caused Hays considerable anxiety because the amounts claimed were large and because it implied dishonorable conduct on the part of his firm and Untermyer. The matter was settled by the payment of $7,500.

In the depressed market of 1933, the five residuary charities did not want to sell the Wendel real estate. Yet how could over 175 parcels in four different states be managed in a businesslike fashion? The solution was the Wendel Foundation, a tax-exempt corporation to be formed under an act passed by the New York state legislature. The sole objection to the act came from Senator MacNaboe, celebrated for stalking alleged "Reds" in the 1930s, who called it an "inconceivable effrontery, a fraud." This charge had no more merit than his Communist witch hunts, since the Foundation would pay real estate taxes just as the Wendel family had. After World War II, when real estate values rose again, the Foundation sold the properties and each of the residuary charities has set up a Wendel fund with the proceeds.

Harlan continued to receive letters for years after the settlement agreement. In October 1933, Mary F. Burkett of Casper, Wyoming, wrote to ask for Thomas Patrick Morris's address, since she wanted to help him prove his claim. She explained that her father, Patrick Kiely, had worked for John G. and had told her of a letter he received from John G. about his marriage to Mary Ellen Devine, with whom Kiely had previously "kept company." Harlan with a straight face gave her the address of the penitentiary on Welfare Island.

The Hays-Untermyer pooling agreement generated additional correspondence. Local attorneys for sixth-degree claimants around the country wrote to Harlan after the newspaper publicity that many sixth-degree claimants received substantial sums. Why, they asked, shouldn't their clients share in the settlement also? Harlan referred all these inquiries to Hays for reply.

Still new claimants surfaced, anxious to file and to share in Ella's fortune. Harlan had the unpleasant task of informing them that their claims came too late. Their responses were often indignant, as though somehow he was personally responsible for their prior failure to file. The letters persisted even up to 1943. One came from Ernst Carl Wendel, who had maintained that Ella's grandfather was an impostor. He was still convinced that was the truth.

> Patience is a virtue, and truth is mightier than bullets. This you should know from experience in business. You have nothing to fear from an honest man, as long as you keep to your obligations, towards the real and legal heirs of John Daniel Wendel. Twelve long years have passed that I gave you a free hand to untangle the dirty work which has been committed against the family, and whereas I have been the only member who met the family of John Daniel Wendel, on board ship in 1895, and had a long conversation with Rebecca Wendel Swope, who was then on her wedding trip with Dr. Luther Swope, to whom she was married between July 20 and 25th, as far as I can remember. This was aboard the S. S. St. Louis in the dining salon on August 9th, when Becky revealed to me that your grandfather, John Marshall Harlan, then a Supreme Court Justice and Ellihu [sic] Root were the trustees of the estate in perpetuity, to protect the family from trouble and want.
>
> Now, however, I feel that I must act and wake up the American people that our Courts and Legislatures are perhaps crooked and not to be trusted and shall demand a public investigation into this matter. If you are still the guardian of the Estate's heirs, I request that you send me the Deed of the Cemetery where the family are resting, as it was Rebecca's wish that all of us should be buried together. I request you also to commence procedure against the so-called Wendel Foundation for $500,000,000. for infringing on the Wendel name. This foundation has not the sanction of the heirs to use the name in the disposal of the loot which has been acquired apparently with the complicity of the corrupt Surrogate Court.
>
> I am sorry that you have at all times evaded meeting me personally, may I ask why? I am human and do not care for wealth personally, but I am bound under oath to Rebecca that I would fight for the rights of the family under all circumstances,

no matter how black the outlook. You will understand that I am only interested that the Wills and Testaments of the founders G.M. and John Daniel will be carried out as provided. Rebecca told me that they were only the holders or tenants of the Estate. As the estate was deeded to my Great grandfather John Wendel of Stralsund.

Hoping to hear from you favorably, and wishing you well,

Nearly twenty years after the settlement, echoes of Ella's will were audible in the Surrogate Court. The Board of Foreign Missions of the Methodist Episcopal Church had received 35/200ths of the residue in both Ella's and Rebecca's estates, to be used for "the maintenance of the Nankin [sic] Theological Seminary." In 1952, the Board told the court:

In the fall term of 1948, the seminary had a faculty of twenty-five, of which about eighteen were full-time instructors, and a student body of one hundred thirty. The occupation of the City of Nanking by the Chinese-Communist Armies in April, 1949, affected the seminary adversely and some of the faculty members withdrew, but the seminary continued with a reduced student body. The seminary opened for the fall term of 1950 with about sixty students.

After the entrance of the Chinese "volunteers" into Korea in October, 1950, and their active engagement with the United Nations forces, a wave of anti-American feeling and propaganda swept through China, which made it difficult or impossible for the American faculty members to continue their work. Upon information and belief, the Chinese authorities forbade the Chinese Christian leaders to associate with American missionaries or faculty members. As a result of this hostility, the American members of the faculty of Nanking Theological Seminary withdrew and by April, 1951, the last one had left China. . . .

When last heard of the seminary was in operation under a Chinese faculty. Communication with the faculty, or with any Chinese who is or was connected with the seminary, has become

> impossible for the reason that a Chinese who was in communication with friends in this country would be suspect of friendliness toward the United States and hostility to the present government of China, and would be subject to harassment and possible prosecution.

And so the board requested permission from the Surrogate—(Foley had died in the interim)—under the cy-pres [as near as (possible)] doctrine, to rechannel the money to ten theological schools in Asia and to provide for the translation of Christian classics for the 20 million Chinese Christians outside of mainland China. The petition was granted, but the Surrogate's Court files do not show whether any of the ten theological schools was in Vietnam, Laos, or Cambodia, where the Communist influence has caused further problems.

24.

ELLA'S WISHES UNFUL-FILLED: WHAT MIGHT HAVE BEEN

"Had I been Present at the Creation I would have given some useful hints for the better ordering of the universe."
KING ALFONSO X,
THE LEARNED, OF SPAIN 1252–1284

JOHN G.'S ILLEGITIMATE SON

John G. did have an illegitimate son. He was a man of strong carnal appetites, but not with women whom he considered his social equals. In the best lord-of-the-manor tradition, he was addicted to dalliance with the servant girls in Quogue and at 442. These poor girls were dazzled by his wealth; being uneducated, they were probably enchanted by his declarations of love in French, German, and Latin; and they were probably afraid of losing their jobs if they refused to come to his bed.

In connection with the Morris claim, Diaz told Harlan (who told Ray Shelton) that on numerous occasions he had been instructed to send the metal sitz bath, along with five pounds of mustard, to Quogue or to 442—a mustard bath being the accepted way to induce an abortion in those less permissive days. But the fetus of one of the servants, whom I will call Mary Smith, did not respond to the mustard bath and in due course a son, "Thomas Smith," was born. The other Wendel servants knew of the birth, and in the course of preparing for the hearings, Wise, Morris's lawyer, discovered it too. He asked Harlan to stipulate to the fact of this son so that he would not have to prove it. But Harlan refused to admit the existence of the illegitimate son, much less to concede its relevance to the Morris claim. Still, in his thorough fashion, he had a memorandum of law prepared, to be used if needed, showing John G.'s promiscuity to be unrelated to the case. After all, Morris claimed to have been born in wedlock.

During his cross-examination, Wise asked Selden Hallock, the owner of the Quogue House, whether he had heard of Mary Smith. Hallock said that he had.

WISE: Did she ever say anything to you about the parent of her son, or did her husband?

HARLAN: I object to the question as irrelevant.

FOLEY: (*to Wise*): What is the purpose of the question?

WISE: If John G. had one child, he might have had another.

FOLEY: I never heard that principle of law argued in any Court. I direct that line of questioning be dropped.

Mary Smith was a decent person and so was Thomas. Alfonso the Learned would have given John G. the useful hint to marry her. Instead, in the same lord-of-the-manor tradition, John G. pressed Mary Smith to marry an upstanding local tradesman, whom he helped set up in business a thousand miles away. But John G. remained fond of Mary and his son and visited them on occasion.

If he had married Mary, notwithstanding the fact that she was not of his "class," the family holdings might have remained intact after Ella's death. For "Thomas," and in turn his children and his children's children, with training at Wharton or the Harvard Business School, might still be operating the largest real estate empire in New York—perhaps the United States—worth many billions of dollars.

Charles Edgar, Nurse Gordon, and the other witnesses who testified about John G.'s allusions to a son or such statements as, "You ought to see my big boy," were probably telling the truth. But to the extent they embroidered their testimony with references to Morris, or about his son in Scotland, they were motivated by desire for publicity more than desire for accuracy.

THE GIFT OF IRVINGTON TO ISABEL KOSS

As she told Koss, Ella wanted to leave Irvington to Stanley Shirk rather than to Isabel, who would "probably marry, go off to Europe, and never live in or take an interest in the place." Koss replied that Isabel would never marry. When Ella reported the exchange to Annie Gavin, she added, "Wait and see if she doesn't." And indeed, Ella was a true prophet, for Isabel married Joseph Murray seven months after Ella died.

Contrary to the prophecy, Isabel did reside in Irvington until her death in 1965, at the age of eighty-one. However, she did not live in the Wendel family home, which she had demolished in 1936. The new house, built in 1938, was occupied by her husband until his death in 1975. Then it was sold, along with ten acres of land, to Griffen International, a construction-design firm that still maintains its office there today. The O'Dell Tavern, built in the 1670s, the fourth oldest structure in New York State, was a stagecoach stop on the old Albany Post Road; it is still standing in one corner of the property. The rest of the land was sold to developers, who erected condominiums.

Ella's animal graveyard, with its underground vaults, is preserved under a large tree by the corner of the terrace. Isabel kept many cats, and she buried them there as well. We do not know what the various Tobeys think of that.

THE GIFT OF 442 FIFTH AVENUE TO DREW THEOLOGICAL SEMINARY

It was Ella's "earnest wish," in willing the house to Drew, that it be maintained "as a memorial to my father John D. and not be disposed of." She had discussed with Koss the possibility of requiring Drew to hold the property and prohibiting its disposal. Koss argued her out of it—if Drew could be compelled to hold on to 442, Isabel could be compelled to retain the house and acreage at Irvington. Fruitlessly, Ella restated her desire to Warren, Koss's partner, at the time of the execution of her will.

Alfonso the Learned would have given Ella the useful hint to consult an independent lawyer to advise her how to accomplish her wishes. The furniture and the 157 trunks were promptly moved out to Madison, New Jersey. In 1934 the mansion was demolished, and Drew leased the large corner plot to S. H. Kress to build a competitor store to the nearby Woolworths. It is now part of the new office building of the Republic National Bank.

TOBEY

Before making her will, Ella told Annie to live at Irvington with Tobey until Tobey died, adding, "Let everything go just as it is now." When Ella expressed this wish to Koss, she told Annie that Koss had "prevented her from making this provision," saying Isabel, who "loved dogs," would take care of Tobey. Ella was very unhappy because she foresaw great trouble between Tobey and Isabel's seven cats. "Tobey's eyes will be scratched out."

Contrary to Koss's promise, Isabel didn't take care of Tobey. He lost his privileged position, along with his four-poster bed and his velvet-covered table. He was consigned to the kitchen of 442, where he stayed with the caretaker.

Three months after Ella's death, the temporary administrators paid $17 to a veterinary hospital for four calls and medicine for Tobey. In September 1931 he was treated again for eczema. Shortly thereafter, to end his suffering, Tobey was put to sleep.

THE NEGLIGENCE OF KOSS IN NOT FINDING ROSA DEW STANSBURY BEFORE ELLA DIED

Alfonso the Learned certainly would have given Koss the useful hint to find Ella's nearest relatives many years before Rebecca and Ella died. Ella had stated, according to Koss, that she had no relatives. But Koss was negligent in accepting that assertion at face value. The Wendel family Bible and that of Rebecca Swope both show Mary Ann Dew the Amiable and her Stansbury connection. Indeed only five months after Ella's death, Rosa Dew Stansbury signed her waiver of citation and consent to probate of Ella's will. If Koss had found Rosa Dew Stansbury while Ella and Rebecca were alive, there would have been no blaze of publicity upon their deaths. Perhaps the eight Barney claimants would have been unearthed, or perhaps not. The 2,303 claimants would not have surfaced to fight for the fortune of the woman "without heirs." And Ella's estate would be richer by the $2 million spent in legal and investigative fees and the $2½ million paid in settlements to avoid the will contest on the claims of the 2,303. But then, the Author hastens to add, this book would not have been written.